Accelerated Product Development

Combining Lean and Six Sigma for Peak Performance

Clifford Fiore

Productivity Press
NEW YORK, NEW YORK

Most Productivity Press books are available at quantity discounts when purchased in bulk. For more information contact our Customer Service Department (888-319-5852). Address all other inquires to:

Productivity Press
444 Park Avenue South, Suite 604
New York, NY 10016
United States of America
Telephone: 212-686-5900
Fax: 212-686-5411
E-mail: info@productivityinc.com

Composition by William H. Brunson Typography Services

Library of Congress Cataloging-in-Publication Data

Fiore, Clifford, 1960–
Accelerated product development : combining lean and six sigma for peak performance / Clifford Fiore.
p. cm.
Includes bibliographical references.
ISBN 1-56327-310-1 (alk. paper)
1. New products. 2. Six sigma (Quality control standard) 3. Production management. I. Title.

TS170.F5 2004
658.5'75—dc22

2004021511

09 08 07 06 05 5 4 3 2 1

To my wife Deidre,
my sons Kendall, Donovan, and Bradley,
and to those individuals who are not bound
by the perceived limitations of their
own abilities and who strive to
conquer new challenges

Table of Contents

Acknowledgments

Throughout my professional career I've had the privilege of working with many talented people. The results of these relationships have been rewarding, not only for the pleasure of working side by side with these individuals to accomplish common goals, but also for the wisdom, experiences, and guidance these individuals have shared with me. The knowledge and lessons I learned from these people have been a major influence in my continuing career and were instrumental in enabling me to write this book. To these individuals I am eternally grateful.

I also wish to extend a special note of gratitude to Dale Jensen, my mentor and former manager, for his continued support and work in the area of improving product development processes. Dale's wealth of experience, coupled with his vision for the future of product development, was the inspiration of many of the ideas presented in this book.

Introduction

The cost pressures facing companies have never been greater than they are today. With the intense competition that exists in today's business environment, the key discriminator for the most successful companies is the ability to provide products to the marketplace quickly and cheaply. Consequently, the lifeblood of many companies rests in the product development processes that enable a company to provide a continual stream of new products that are better, cheaper, and reach the customer faster than the competition.

Improving the product development process is a significant challenge for many companies; yet, it also represents a significant opportunity. Companies that are successful in providing low-cost, high-quality products to their customers, in the shortest time possible, will undoubtedly realize a competitive advantage that will reap rewards of greater market share and improved profitability.

Over the last decade, we've seen companies apply lean and six sigma methodologies in factories to generate a competitive advantage and, in many cases, they have achieved significant results. For example, many companies have embraced and adopted the philosophy of the much-publicized Toyota Production System. However, across industry, there's an emerging trend of companies expressing a desire to apply lean and six sigma concepts outside of manufacturing. Companies are realizing that as the bar continues to rise in terms of customer expectations and demands, they need to respond by looking beyond the factory floor in order to continue to make improvements and maintain a competitive advantage.

If you look across industry in general, the application of lean and six sigma concepts in the area of product development is virtually an untapped opportunity. However, companies that have focused on their product development process and applied the lean and six sigma concepts that will be presented in this book have achieved some dramatic results. In some cases, reductions of 60 to 70 percent in product development cycle time have been achieved.

Accelerated Product Development highlights problems that are common to companies in terms of developing products cheaply and efficiently, and it represents one of the first books in industry to couple the proven concepts of lean and six sigma with engineering processes dealing with product development. The result is a book, based on proven strategies and methodologies, that will enable a company to significantly reduce the time necessary to develop new products, dramatically reduce product cost, and improve product quality.

Accelerated Product Development is intended to be an extension of and complementary to my first book entitled *Lean Strategies for Product Development: Achieving Breakthrough Performance in Bringing Product to Market.* Where *Lean Strategies* is intended to be a short business novel introducing readers to the application of lean concepts and fundamentals within product development, *Accelerated Product Development* provides the blueprint and outlines key elements for improving the product development process through lean and six sigma methodologies. The material is presented in a sequence that is a roadmap for implementation and is based on proven results that will maximize the benefits for a company.

Part One provides information that will give the reader insight into the scope and magnitude of the opportunity that exists in the product development arena. In addition, this section will introduce some basic lean concepts and demonstrate specifically how these concepts relate to product development.

Part Two discusses the approach for launching improvement in the product development process. This section will present the methodology for assessing a company's current process and developing a plan for improvement.

Part Three presents information to stabilize the product development process. This section introduces concepts that represent the foundational elements for process improvement in product development.

Part Four is devoted to streamlining the product development process. The elements introduced in this section focus heavily on reducing development cycle time and product cost through the design process selection, as well as manufacturing and supply chain integration.

Part Five provides information to improve product quality in the development process. This section focuses on elements that utilize product data in order to understand the capability of processes that can be used to improve quality levels.

The book is aimed towards business management leaders, engineering leaders in industry, and practitioners of the product development, engineering, manufacturing, and supply chain disciplines. Company vice presidents, general managers, engineering leaders, and supply chain managers will benefit from this material by using it to shape a new product development vision and supply chain strategy for their company. Practitioners will benefit by understanding the key elements and by gaining insight into the step-by-step methodology by which real and lasting improvement in their product development processes can be made.

Product development is the next frontier for many companies and an area ripe for improvement. As a result of working in this arena for the last eight years, I have been able to employ the concepts presented in this book and see firsthand the improvements that can be made. As a certified black belt and lean expert, coupled with my years of experience in design, manufacturing, process improvement, and quality improvement, I have learned to appreciate the power in combining lean and six sigma in order to increase productivity and company profit.

Through this book, I invite you to undertake this same journey, and learn how to apply lean and six sigma methodologies in product development to increase profitability in your company!

Clifford Fiore

PART ONE

The Product Development Value Proposition

Part One outlines the opportunities for focusing on product development, introduces lean fundamentals, and shows how these concepts relate to the product development process.

CHAPTER 1

Why Focus on Product Development?

The current environment in which we conduct business is more intense and dynamic than it has ever been. Clearly, today we live in a world of rising expectations. As we continue to move forward in the global economy and competition continues to increase, customers' needs are also increasing. This is not an issue that affects only certain industries; rather, it's an issue that has an impact on all businesses. Today's information age provides customers with access to more kinds of knowledge and information about products and markets than were ever explored before. With this access, customers are afforded the luxury of being highly selective in the products they purchase, resulting in an intensely competitive business environment.

Consequently, customers are demanding price reductions in the products they purchase. They're looking for improvements in on-time delivery and shorter cycle times in developing and bringing products to market. They want their products to work right with low maintenance costs, and, finally, they're looking for a variety of products that match their changing needs. For these reasons, it's fair to conclude that today's customers are clearly more demanding than they've ever been.

So what effect do these ever-increasing demands have on companies that provide products to these customers? For companies to remain competitive, they must respond and adapt to the changing environment. Consequently, the needs of companies are also changing. In today's world, companies are looking at how to produce products with shorter development cycle times, and, correspondingly, lower development costs. They're looking for ways to improve program control that enable them to consistently meet delivery and schedule commitments. And they're looking for ways to maintain their profit margins in light of the cost concessions mandated by their customers. In addition, the global movement towards trade agreements and more open markets has provided companies and their competitors with access to larger and cheaper labor pools, which has induced additional pressures to reduce costs.

In conjunction with a company's overall needs, factory needs are also changing, whether it is a manufacturing facility within a company or external suppliers representing a company's supply chain. Factories are looking to manufacture products that represent simpler, more producible designs. In addition, they're looking to companies to support cost take-out and cost reduction opportunities that align with the philosophy of continuous improvement.

So what opportunities truly exist in the area of product development? Companies spend huge amounts of money in developing products; and in many cases the effort does not culminate in the creation of products that provide a monetary return or benefit for the company. Over the years, many studies have been conducted that support this claim. For example, according to Booz, Allen & Hamilton, 46 percent of all product development costs go into failures. The process of developing products is complex and is influenced by many factors, including customer needs, market trends, cost, technology, timing of product introduction, and good old-fashioned human creativity and innovation among others. Nonetheless, regardless of which set of numbers you believe from the multitude of research studies that have been conducted, a common theme is clear. A major opportunity exists for companies to improve the effectiveness of their product development process, in terms of managing both the process of creating viable products that benefit the company, and the associated costs in developing products.

THE RELATIONSHIP OF PRODUCT DEVELOPMENT AND PRODUCT COST

Let's further explore the opportunities in product development by examining the relationship between a company's cost in developing products and the actual product cost. As shown in Figure 1-1, the solid line represents the percentage of cost that a company incurs in developing a product, and the dashed line represents the actual cost of the product.

As illustrated by Figure 1-1, a large percentage of the actual product cost is locked in very early in the product development process. For example, during the concept phase, where a company has invested less than 5 percent of the total development cost, approximately 50 percent of the actual product cost is committed. As the process evolves into the design phase, nearly 70

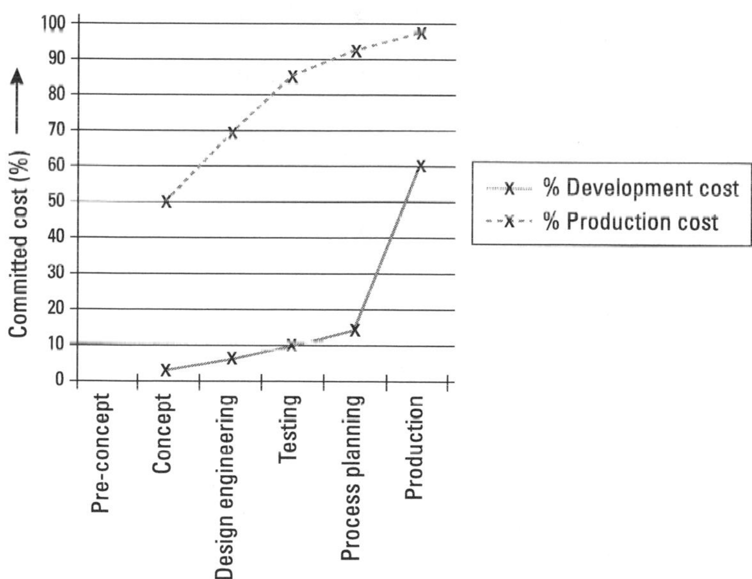

Figure 1-1. Impact of Product Design on Cost

percent of the product cost is locked in. Clearly, the product development process has significant influence on the product's cost.

Many Japanese companies (as well as other proponents of the concept of concurrent engineering) have long recognized this issue. Although the largest percentage of product cost is established in the early stages of the product development process, this is also the time when the product design has the greatest degree of flexibility. Consequently, the product-development phase represents the best opportunity to make significant changes that influence issues down stream, such as manufacturing and product serviceability. By addressing these issues early, the company can minimize the impact of costly changes later on in the process after investments have been made in creating detailed drawings, fabricating tooling, and so forth.

THE EVOLUTION OF CONTINUOUS IMPROVEMENT

Let's summarize the opportunity for focusing on product development by looking at the evolution of the various continuous improvement initiatives shown in Figure 1- 2. In addition, let's review the elements implemented to date and explain why the timing is now right to focus on the product development process.

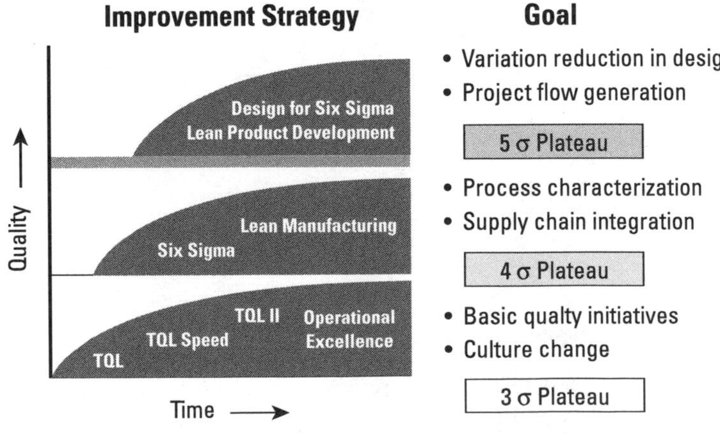

Figure 1-2. Evolution of Continuous Improvement

Phase 1: Total Quality Leadership

In the early 1990s, companies were introduced to the whole concept of continuous improvement through an initiative know as total quality leadership or TQL. This philosophy and its many versions armed workers with some basic tools in dealing with process improvement and laid the foundation for changing a company's culture in dealing with continuous improvement. For many companies and their employees, TQL represented the first exposure to tools such as brainstorming, cause-and-effect diagrams, and Pareto charts. Through the use of tools such as process mapping and fishbone diagrams, TQL challenged employees to question existing company processes in order to reduce cycle time and increase efficiency. In addition, TQL taught companies to consider the impact of their activities beyond their own walls, both in terms of providing real value to the customer and the effects of their actions on their suppliers. For many companies, the business improvements made as a result of their TQL initiative helped them break through the three sigma quality barrier.

Phase 2: Six Sigma and Lean Manufacturing

During the mid-1990s, we saw the emergence of the six sigma and lean initiatives in the manufacturing arena. These initiatives continued to build on the TQL philosophy and took quality and cost improvements to a new level. Six sigma focused heavily on variation reduction through statistical analysis for factory-related issues. Additional goals of six sigma included rework/scrap elimination and process characterization and control. Conversely, the lean manufacturing initiative focused on waste elimination and reducing cycle time in the factory. It embraced the concepts of single-piece flow, understanding true customer value, and eliminating non-value-added tasks. Collectively, these initiatives helped companies break through the four sigma quality barrier.

Phase 3: The Focus on Product Design and Development

In light of today's business climate, companies recognize that they must look in other areas to remain competitive. Many companies have exhausted the benefits of focusing in the manufacturing arena and are realizing that in order to break through the five sigma barrier and achieve world class status, they must now focus in other areas. For example, the factory-focused six sigma initiative that many companies employed in the 1990s has given way to a new engineering-focused initiative known as *Design for Six Sigma*. Similarly, the successful gains made in manufacturing using lean concepts has led to a desire by many companies to apply lean concepts beyond the factory walls; that is, in administrative and other office-related processes, including product development. Companies are now realizing that improvements made in the inherent design of the product through initiatives like lean product development and Design for Six Sigma will enable dramatic reductions in product cost and time to market, resulting in a significant competitive advantage.

LEAN AND SIX SIGMA

As we embark on the journey of applying lean and six sigma in product development, it is important to understand the relationship between the lean and six sigma methodologies and the benefits that are derived from each. Referring to Figure 1-3, we see that the objectives of lean and six sigma are indeed different, but complementary.

The lean philosophy uses the concepts of value streams, waste elimination, work concentration, and flow to meet the goal of reduced cycle time. Conversely, the six sigma methodology uses variation reduction, rework and scrap elimination, and process control to improve product quality. In addition, characteristics of improvement projects based on lean concepts within a company tend to be systemic or process-based, while projects focused on six sigma tend to be (individually) product-based. The important point for companies undertaking any continuous improvement initiative is to first determine the goal, and then to adopt and apply the appropriate strategy in order to achieve the goal.

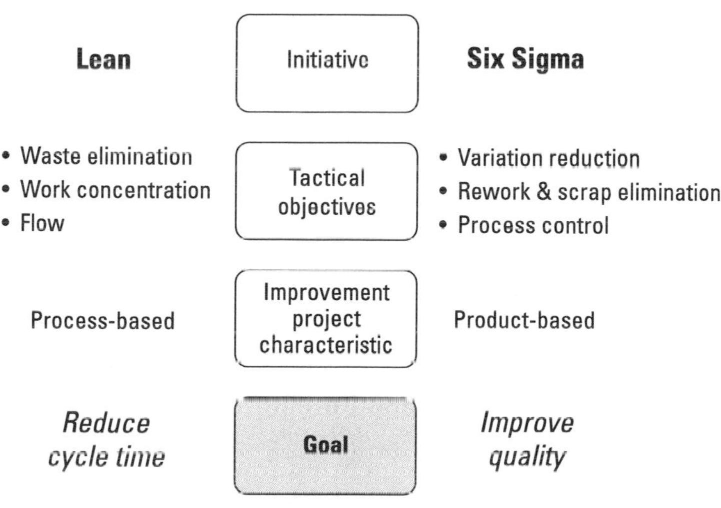

Figure 1-3. Lean and Six Sigma

Chapter 2 introduces the fundamentals of the lean philosophy, which will be used as the basis for reducing cycle time in the product development process.

CHAPTER 2

Lean Fundamentals

Let's begin the discussion of lean concepts by starting with the basic definition of lean. If you look in any dictionary, the typical definition of lean is something that contains little fat, or something that is severely curtailed or reduced:

> **lean** (lēn) *adj.* **1.** Not fleshy or fat; thin. **2.** Containing little or no fat. **3. a.** Not productive or prosperous. **b.** Severely curtailed or reduced.

Translating this definition of lean into the business world, lean means producing what is needed, when it is needed, with the minimum amount of materials, equipment, labor, and space. In other words, producing what is required and when it is required, but with minimal investment.

So, what is the objective of a company or business that wants to be lean? Essentially, the goal of a company adopting the lean philosophy is to make each process as efficient and effective as possible, and then to connect those processes in a stream or continuous chain that is focused on flow and maximizing customer value. Figure 2-1 provides a high-level structure of a lean business enterprise. Relating these terms to a business, what is really meant by "flow" and "maximizing customer value"? To answer this question, let's take a closer look at each one.

THE CONCEPT OF FLOW

Everyone can relate to the concept of *flow* if we use the example of water flowing continuously through a stream or river in

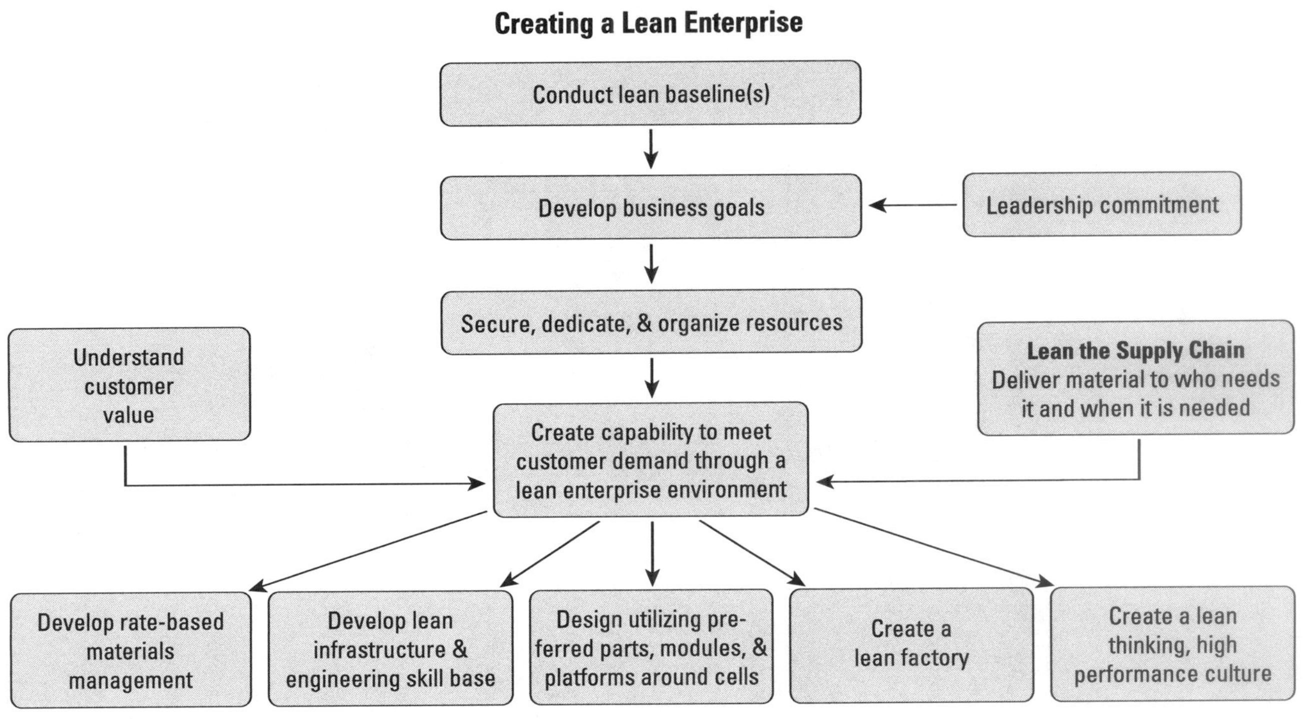

Figure 2-1. Lean Enterprise Structure

nature. Similar to this example, flow in the business world refers to the continuous movement of products and information through a value stream. Relating this to the objective for a lean enterprise, the goal here is to minimize idle time, which really equates to inefficiency and waste.

If you think about it, there are many examples that demonstrate the concept of flow that we can see in everyday life. To illustrate this concept, let's use a case study that compares two sandwich companies: the ACME Sandwich Company and the Subworld Sandwich Shop.

Both companies offer a variety of sandwiches to their customers, a modest selection of soft drinks, chips and snacks, and the option of dine-in service. However, ACME and Subworld take different approaches in preparing and providing sandwiches to their customers.

ACME's process for making sandwiches is to prepare batches of the different sandwiches it offers at various times throughout the course of the day, to have them readily available for customers. In preparing sandwiches using this approach, the entire batch moves from station to station. For example, the first step in making a sandwich is to cut the bread. Consequently, bread for the entire batch is cut. Then, the sandwich batch moves to the second step to add the meat. The batch then proceeds to the next station to add the toppings, followed by the condiments, and, finally, sandwiches are individually packaged and placed on a shelf to await purchase.

Subworld's process contains the same basic elements but takes a different approach in preparing their sandwiches. Their process of making sandwiches does not begin until a customer enters the shop and places an order. With Subworld's approach, the customer views the entire sandwich-making process. In addition, the customer can select the toppings he or she would like on the sandwich and in what quantity. When the condiments are added, once again the customer can select the ones he or she wants and in the amount preferred. Finally, the sandwich is packaged and handed to the customer to pay the cashier.

Company #1: Batch Production

In order to fully appreciate the impact of flow regarding the two sandwich companies, it is necessary to look at flow from the perspective of the product, in this case, the individual sandwich. In ACME's case, because of the batch approach in preparing sandwiches, nearly all of the time that each sandwich spends in the process is represented as idle time. Let's illustrate this point with the following information related to ACME's process.

Let's assume a batch contains 25 sandwiches and the time for each task is depicted in Figure 2-2.

Task	Time/Sandwich
Cut Bread	20 seconds
Add Meat	15 seconds
Add Toppings	30 seconds
Add Condiments	30 seconds
Packaging	15 seconds
Total Time	**110 seconds**

Figure 2-2. ACME's Task Time in Sandwich Preparation

The initial task of cutting the bread takes 20 seconds for each sandwich, but because we're making a batch of 25 sandwiches, the total time required to complete the breading cutting task is:

20 seconds/sandwich × 25 sandwiches = 500 seconds
(or about 8 1/2 minutes)

From the perspective of the first sandwich cut in the batch, only 20 seconds is needed. It is then ready to move on to the next step. But, because the sandwich is part of a batch, it must wait an additional 8 minutes (480 seconds) for the other sandwiches to be completed. For the next task of adding meat, 15 seconds is truly needed for each sandwich, but it takes a total of 6-1/4 minutes (375 seconds) in order to complete the entire batch. If we include the toppings and condiments, the total time to complete the batch for these three tasks is more than 31 minutes (1875 seconds). Including the packaging task, we see that the total time to complete the first sandwich using a batch method takes over 39 minutes (2390 seconds, see Figure 2-3). In other words, although it takes less than two minutes of actual process time to prepare a sandwich, ACME's batch mode approach takes more than 39 minutes for the first complete sandwich to come through the process! Each additional sandwich comes out of the packaging process step at 15-second intervals (note: in this example we have excluded the time in moving the batch from one station to the next).

What is the real significance of these numbers? From the perspective of waste, although the actual processing time to make a sandwich is less than 2 minutes (110 seconds), in the case of the first sandwich, it spends almost 40 minutes (2390 seconds) in a process of which 38 minutes (2280 seconds) is idle time. In other words, each sandwich in ACME's process spends a minimum of 95 percent of its time in the process with nothing done to it!

Company #2: Single-Piece Flow

Subworld's approach is much simpler to assess. Because it operates on a customized approach by initiating the sandwich-making process only when a customer order is received, it is not burdened with the in-process wait times for the product that is characterized by ACME's approach. Consequently, once the creation of the sandwich is initiated with the first task of bread cutting, the product is able to flow through the subsequent tasks with no wait time associated with the batch

Sandwich Number	**Cut Bread**		Time to Add Meat, Toppings, Condiments (Seconds)	**Packaging**		Total Time to Complete Sandwich (Seconds)
	Process Time (Seconds)	Wait Time (Seconds)		Process Time (Seconds)	Wait Time (Seconds)	
Sandwich 1	20	480	1875	15	0	2390

Figure 2-3. ACME's Batch Approach for Completing First Sandwich

approach. Therefore, Subworld's total processing time following this approach is equivalent to 110 seconds, or less than 2 minutes. This process is a good example demonstrating the concept of single-piece flow.

Batch vs. Single-Piece Flow = Push vs. Pull

It is important to add a few comments of clarification to this overly simplistic case study. The two sandwich companies utilize processes that represent different ends of the spectrum related to product flow: ACME's pure batch system essentially represents no flow, whereas Subworld's single-piece processing approach represents total flow. In addition, a number of factors that could potentially influence the process time in our example include resource levels, material availability, and work-in-process inventory levels among others.

However, from the perspective of flow, hopefully you can see that there are some real and inherent problems associated with operating in a pure batch mode. From a customer's perspective, ACME's approach in preparing sandwiches is essentially independent of any real customer demand. This is an example of a *push* system, defined as follows:

> A push system completes a predetermined quantity of work from an established work queue or forecast. Typically, the work queue or forecast is offset to the actual customer demand to allow time for production and delivery.

ACME's approach is also characterized by high levels of inventory. Once complete, the sandwich is placed on a shelf to wait for a buyer. Following this approach, ACME is banking on its ability to sell its pre-made sandwiches and is assuming a high degree of risk. In reality, how long do you think ACME could remain in business using this business model if it had to continuously throw away inventories of pre-made sandwiches?

Conversely, Subworld operates using a *pull* system. In this case, the process of creating a sandwich is triggered only when a customer order initiates the process. The customer creates the pull, or need, that directly drives the activities of the process to satisfy the need. A pull system is defined as the following:

> A pull system completes a quantity of work that is directly linked to customer demand. Materials are staged at the point of consumption. As materials are consumed, signals are sent to previous steps in the process to pull forward sufficient materials to replenish only those that have been consumed.

Clearly, based on the numbers associated with wait-time in our example, Subworld employs a process in which the product flows, whereas ACME uses an approach that does not. But this is not intended to imply that certain characteristics of ACME's business model do not have merit. For example, for customers that are in a hurry, ACME's approach of having ready-made sandwiches might be preferable to Subworld's approach, where the customer must wait for the sandwich to be made. Ultimately, selection of the business model to be implemented should be dictated by marketplace demands with the goal of maximizing value for the customer.

MAXIMIZING CUSTOMER VALUE

As just stated, the appropriate business model is one that attempts to maximize customer value. To introduce this topic, let's define customer value. Simply stated, customer value refers to specific activities that add value to the products and services that customers buy. The important point to note here is that the determination of what is value-added is made from the customer's perspective, that is, the customer's point of view, not the company's.

Under the lean philosophy, for an activity to be *value-added*, it must meet the following three criteria:

1. The customer must be willing to pay for the activity.
2. The part or object must change.
3. It must be done right the first time.

Let's expand on the meaning of each.

First, the customer must be willing to pay for the activity. This is pretty straightforward. If a customer perceives something is important and is willing to pay for it, in the customer's eyes it has value.

Second, the part or object must change or be altered in some way. For example, consider the movement of parts from one machine to another, a work order form being routed from one department to the next, parts that are stored, or any inspection operation. These activities do not change the product in any way that will benefit the customer. Consequently, they are not considered value-added activities.

And third, the activity must be done right the first time. If the activity is not performed correctly, the customer certainly will not be willing to pay for it, and additional time, effort, and money will be required to correct or replace the product. Once again, for an activity to be value-added, all three criteria must be satisfied. Any action that does not meet all three criteria is considered a *non-value-added activity* and represents *waste*.

We can further illustrate the concept of value-added and non-value-added by using a simple example that hopefully everyone can relate to: a football game. A typical football game lasts approximately three hours. It is comprised of four 15-minute quarters, for a total playing time of 60 minutes. When you think about achieving the objective of a football game (which is to score the most points), the true value-added time begins when the ball is hiked and ends when the ball carrier is tackled. If you think back to the three criteria we just reviewed for a value-added activity, all of the other time associated with a football game is essentially non-value-added.

Based on our football game definition of value-added, if you consider that an average play takes about eight seconds and a typical game contains 140 plays, the total value-added time for a football game is about 19 minutes. So for a three-hour game, the true value-added time is less than 11 percent! (See Figure 2-4). The key take-away from this example is that by viewing a process in the context of what is truly value-added, a different perspective will emerge for the opportunities for improvement.

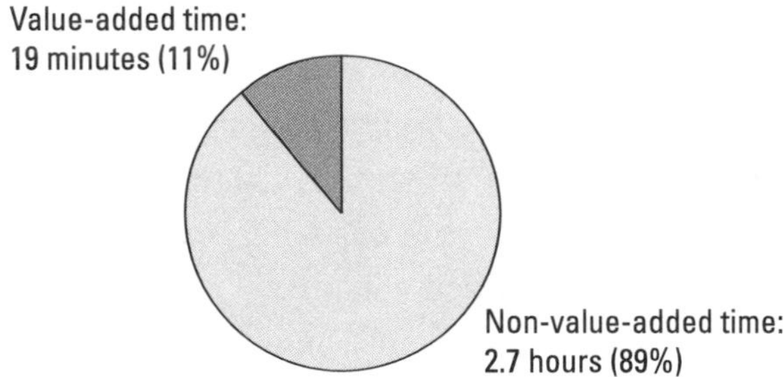

Figure 2-4. Example of Value-Added Time

ELIMINATING WASTE

As noted in the last section, any action that does not meet the three criteria for a value-added activity is considered non-value-added, thereby representing a source of waste and an opportunity for elimination. Under the lean approach, these sources of waste can be grouped in any one of seven different categories. These categories are represented by an acronym known as DOTWIMP, which stands for Defects, Over-production, Transportation, Waiting (the actual waiting time or queue time for the product), Inventory, Motion (referring to the motion of a person), and finally, Processing. Figure 2-5 provides examples of waste associated with each of the seven categories in a traditional manufacturing environment.

Type of Waste	Factory Waste Example
Defects	• Parts Failing Functional Test • Part Feature Violating Blueprint Dimensional Requirement
Over-production	• Machining Parts with No Usage Requirement
Transportation	• Moving Parts from One Machine to Another
Waiting	• Partially Machined Parts on the Shop Floor Queued for the Next Operation
Inventory	• Completed Parts That Have Not Been Purchased
Motion	• Extra Process Steps
Processing	• Part Inspection

Figure 2-5. Waste Categories and Examples

As stated earlier, the goal of a business striving to be lean is to maximize value for the customer. Consequently, the key tenet under the philosophy of lean and continuous improvement is to minimize the non-value-added tasks and eliminate sources of waste represented by these seven categories.

Differentiating Required Waste from Pure Waste

Beyond the seven categories, waste can be further segregated into categories identified as *required waste* and *pure waste*. Required waste represents activities that do not meet the three criteria for a value-added task but are still necessary to support the creation of a product. In addition, required waste is also represented by activities that are mandated by the customer. Placing orders, material requisitioning, and even some inspections operations may fall in this category.

For example, consider an inspection operation to check for cracks on jet engine turbine blades. Regarding the three criteria for a value-added activity, blade inspection is obviously a non-value-added task; it does not alter or change the product in any way, shape, or form. However, due to the criticality of the turbine blades to insure safe operation of the aircraft, the potential impact on human life, and requirements mandated for inspection by government and aviation regulations, the inspection operation is clearly a necessary step.

Pure waste represents those activities that are non-value-added and not required by the customer or necessary for the development of the product. The most obvious example of pure waste (and the largest opportunity for improvement) is associated with the idle time or wait time within a process. Consequently, pure waste activities represent the top priority for elimination.

THE 5S APPROACH FOR LEAN IMPLEMENTATION

Five S (5S) is a methodology to transform and maintain a work environment that supports lean implementation. In addition, it is a methodology that promotes a culture of order and efficiency in the workplace. The term "five S" is derived from five Japanese words (in parentheses below) representing the elements that drive the transformation in the workplace.

1. Sort (*seiri*) means to clearly separate necessary items from the unnecessary. It requires the identification of what is needed to perform a particular operation or task and the removal of unneeded tools, equipment, files, parts, furniture, and so on, from the work area.
2. Store (*seiton*) means to neatly arrange and create a place for each item for ease of use. It requires items to be organized based on the frequency of use. In addition, visual aids are employed to easily identify the needed items.

3. Shine (*seiso*) means to perform daily cleaning and inspection of the equipment and work area.
4. Standardize (*seiketsu*) means to determine, share, and use the best processes and methods. Standardization serves to minimize the variation and becomes the baseline for further improvement.
5. Sustain (*shitsuke*) means to maintain the gains and to create a culture for future improvement. This element supports the philosophy of continuous improvement.

Five S provides the foundation for creating discipline in the workplace. Consequently, 5S implementation is a logical first step in creating a lean business enterprise. However, it has other merits as well. For example, it cultivates relationships in the company and raises employee morale. In addition, work areas that are clean and neat will gain credibility with customers, suppliers, and visitors to the company.

DEFINING VALUE STREAMS

In a lean business enterprise, a *value stream* is simply the connection of process steps with the goal of maximizing customer value. But more specifically, a value stream represents the linkage of all value-added *and* non-value-added activities associated with the creation of a product or service desired by a customer. It begins with the customer having a want or need, and ends with the company providing a product or service that fulfills that need.

Within a company, there can be many value streams. For example, in manufacturing, a value stream can be the production flow of raw material to the completion of the finished product. Or in product development, the value stream could be the information flow of technical requirements to the creation of the drawing package. A value stream exists wherever a company conducts activities that provide value to a customer. The challenge for companies is to become aware of, or see, their value streams.

Fortunately, companies can use a tool known as a *value stream map* to identify and document value streams. Evaluating business processes from the perspective of the value stream is critical in identifying real improvement opportunities related to flow and maximizing customer value.

Figure 2-6 is an example of a value stream map that shows a company's process for evaluating and processing requests for revisions to engineering blueprint drawings. As you can see, the actual process steps are identified by the information denoted in the boxes, for example, *Initiate change order request form*, *Business review*, and so on. There is also a tracking activity performed after each step in the process, denoted by the box entitled *Document Tracking System*. The numbers directly below each process box represent the average process time to complete each process step. The numbers located below the striped arrows represent the lead time, or queue time, for the product at each step in the process. If you notice, there is considerable lead time (more than 13 days on average) for the process step *Prepare change order document*. The numbers below the triangles that contain the capitol letter *I* represent work-in-process (WIP) inventory.

As you can see, the process step, *Prepare change order document*, is once again the main offender with 45 documents in its queue. However, the real impact of using a value stream map is apparent when you sum up the numbers that represent the total process time and production lead time. Referring to the map, the total time for completing a request utilizing the entire process is only 2.75 hours (assuming an 8-hour workday, the processing time hours represent only 1.2 percent of the total leadtime). A key point regarding the 2.75 hours is that it represents both the value-added and non-value-added activities in this process. However, it takes a leadtime of more than 29 days to get a request through the process! If you think about the

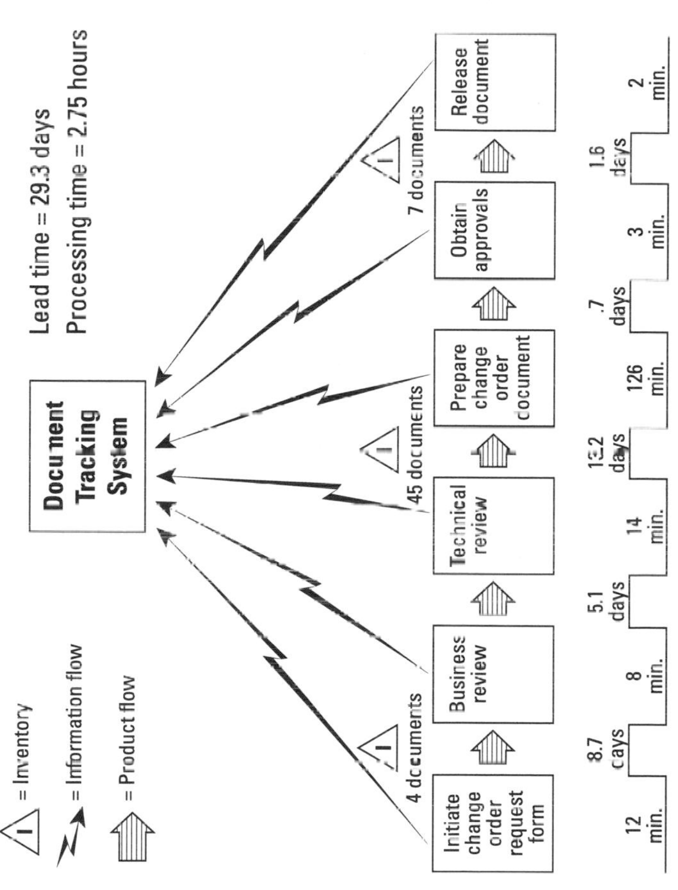

Figure 2-6. Value Stream Map Example

concept of flow in terms of eliminating idle time, those 29 days represent a major opportunity for improvement.

Hopefully, you can begin to see the power in using a value stream map:

- It provides the benefit of visualizing more than just the activities in a process. As demonstrated by this example, it's pretty astounding when you consider the actual process time compared to the overall lead time within a process.
- It helps identify the sources of waste and impediments to flow. In the example, the process step that dealt with preparing the change order document is clearly a bottleneck and impediment to flow: it has a 13-day leadtime and a backlog of 45 documents in its queue.
- It helps identify the information flows as well as the product and material flows in a process. The links between the document tracking system box and the process steps in our example illustrate information flows.
- And finally, a value stream map helps reduce cherry picking of improvement projects.

In summary, a value stream map represents the basis for a continuous improvement plan.

LEAN PRINCIPLES

The topics discussed in this chapter have set the stage for the introduction of the five lean principles. These well-publicized principles embody the philosophy of lean and should be used as the guideposts for developing a lean business enterprise. The five principles are:

1. Specify value in the eyes of the customer.
2. Identify the value stream and eliminate waste.
3. Make value flow at the pull of the customer.

4. Involve and empower employees.
5. Continuously improve in pursuit of perfection.

The last two principles are intended to follow the doctrine of continuous improvement. There is no better source a company has in terms of gaining insight about a specific process or identifying opportunities for improvement than through the employees performing the work. Consequently, employee involvement represents a key ingredient in the development of any improvement plan. Lastly, the principle of improving in pursuit of perfection goes to the heart of the philosophy of continuous improvement, which, essentially, is a never-ending journey.

OPPORTUNITIES FOR PROCESS IMPROVEMENT

To summarize this chapter and highlight the improvement opportunities using lean principles, let's introduce a concept referred to as the "process improvement pitfall" (shown in Figure 2-7). The goal here is to further illustrate the power in viewing process improvement from the perspective of the value stream.

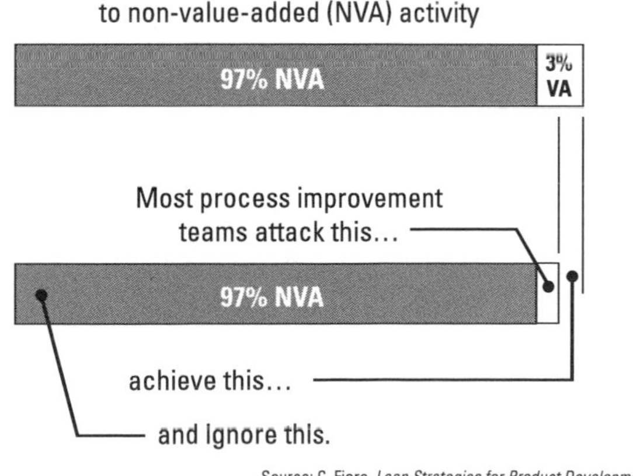

Source: C. Fiore, *Lean Strategies for Product Development*, ASQ, 2003

Figure 2-7. Process Improvement Pitfall

Across industry, if you look at a typical value stream, data indicates that nearly 97 percent of the total time is associated with non-value-added activities, and only 3 percent is associated with adding value for the customer. This is where the pitfall lies. Historically speaking, process improvement teams have tended to evaluate processes by focusing on only those actions where something is being done to the product (essentially the 3 percent portion of the value stream) and virtually ignore the non-value-added activities, such as transportation, queue time, and so on, which represent the 97 percent portion of the value stream. Consequently, most teams tend to focus on a very small portion of the value stream, and miss the larger opportunity to make significant improvement.

The lean concepts and tools discussed in Chapter 2 represent enablers for process improvement. Chapter 3 explores how to apply these enablers to the product development process.

CHAPTER 3

Applying Lean Principles to Product Development

Let's begin this chapter by offering some thoughts related to lean implementation. Historically, the application of lean concepts in manufacturing made perfect sense for many companies. In the past, this represented the area of the largest opportunity for improvement. To date, many companies have successfully utilized lean manufacturing techniques in their factories, including Toyota, GE, Honeywell, Motorola, and Black & Decker, to name a few. In addition, there is extensive literature available related to the topic of lean manufacturing dealing with concepts such as single-piece flow, lean cells, kaizen, and so on. But for reasons we've already stated, lean implementation beyond the factory floor remains a major opportunity.

Regarding the product development process, lean implementation is relatively simple. To clarify, implementation in product development is not analytically complex nor does it require the heavy investment in capital equipment so often required in the manufacturing world. In addition, incremental benefits that are realized can support a pay-as-you-go implementation. Many examples exist of companies that provided seed money for the initial lean product development effort. After realizing some savings through product cost reductions, the money was reinvested for further implementation. Consequently, after the initial investment, the lean implementation became self-sustaining.

On the other hand, lean implementation in product development is not easy. In many companies, the product development process has not changed or been challenged for a long time. In addition, the human factor needs to be considered, due to the natural tendency for people to resist change. However, companies whose management teams embrace the lean philosophy, communicate the vision, and are committed and instrumental in facilitating the lean implementation have achieved rapid and dramatic improvement.

The challenge in adapting lean principles to product development rests on the ability to tailor the existing strategies and techniques. In the factory, processes are centered on producing parts. In this setting, lean-related problems are apparent in many instances simply by viewing the quantity and distribution of parts throughout the facility. Conversely, in product development, processes deal with information and data rather than parts. Consequently, in an office setting, where product development occurs, it's much more difficult to observe and identify issues related to lean principles. As a result, one reason lean principles have not been extensively applied in non-manufacturing processes, such as product development, is because it's easier to observe the flow of parts than the flow of information. As noted in Chapter 2, many companies face the challenge of seeing the value stream.

However, a correlation exists between parts and information. As you can see in Figure 3-1, compared to a factory process that produces parts, the key deliverable of the product development process is focused on providing information. Consequently, activities surrounding the product development process deal with acquiring, transforming, and integrating information.

WASTE IN THE PRODUCT DEVELOPMENT PROCESS

Let's return to the DOTWIMP acronym (introduced in Chapter 2) used in lean methodology to characterize waste (represented by non-value-added activities) and take a look at some exam-

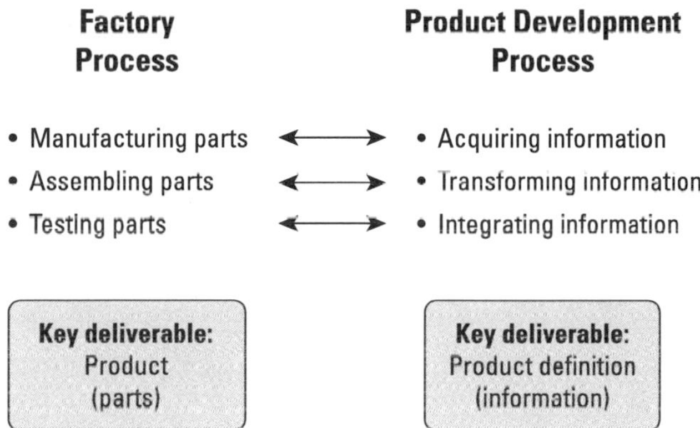

Figure 3-1. Correlation between Factory and Product Development Processes

ples related to product development (see Figure 3-2). As you can see, a different mindset is required when you consider waste in non-manufacturing processes, such as product development. Drawing errors, recreating data, and obtaining approvals are all examples centered on addressing the key deliverable of the product development process, which is to create a product definition through information.

A Case Study

Let's further examine the effect of waste in the product development process by reviewing a case study from a company's process for producing electric switches. The switches are used in a wide variety of commercial and industrial applications. The company's product development process for creating switches is shown in the high-level value stream map in Figure 3-3. Similar to the blueprint drawing revision process shown in Figure 2-6, this process is characterized by high levels of waste. In this case, the total processing time (11.6 hours) represents 4.8 percent of the total leadtime (assuming an 8-hour workday for 30.1 days).

We can take a closer look at the waste by examining the breakdown of value-added and non-value-added activities in a

Type of Waste	Product Development Example
Defects	• Incorrect Data on a Form • Engineering Blueprint Errors
Over-production	• Printing Extra Reports • Designing but Never Producing a Product
Transportation	• Data Hand-Offs • Moving a Form from One Department to Another
Waiting	• A Form in an In Box • Processing Work on a Monthly Basis (Closeouts, Billings, etc.)
Inventory	• Transactions Not Processed • Data that is Not Utilized
Motion	• Unnecessary Analysis • Extra Process Step
Processing	• Approvals, Sign-Offs • Sending or Printing Files Not Requested

Figure 3-2. Product Development Examples of Waste

process by using a tool known as a *time-value map*. This tool provides a comparative assessment of value-added to non-value-added time in a process, and it helps highlight the opportunity for eliminating non-value-added tasks.

From a product development perspective, value-added activities are those that add to the body of knowledge and help define the product that meets the customer's needs. For example, time spent performing calculations of an engineering analysis to determine appropriate material selection or the sizing of components would be a value-added activity. However, activities associated with finding a reference book in a cluttered office area to assist in performing the analysis would be considered waste. Regarding this process, in addition to the activities that define the product design, the assembly of the hardware is also a value-added task. However, the time spent testing and validating the product is non-value-added.

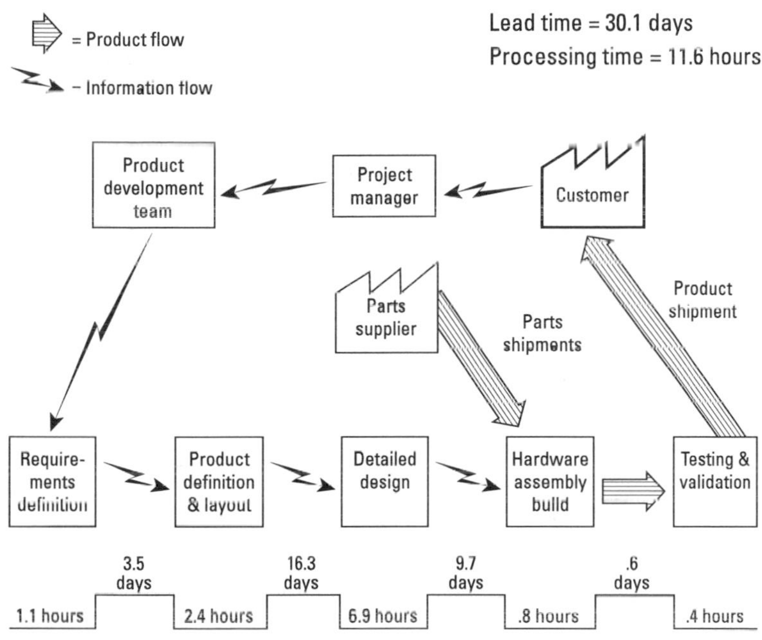

Figure 3-3. Value Stream Map for Developing Switches

Using a Time-Value Map

Referring to the map, the horizontal time line in Figure 3-4 represents the queue time in the process. This line is also used to distinguish the value-added from the non-value-added time. The vertical lines on either side of the horizontal queue line represent the time associated with performing each activity. The thickness of each vertical (activity) line corresponds to the relative time required to complete each task, while the white space between the lines represents idle or wait time.

As you can see, a time-value map is an effective way to graphically represent value-added and non-value-added time within a process. It also represents an effective communication tool for management and other individuals in the organization regarding the opportunities that exist for waste elimination and improvement.

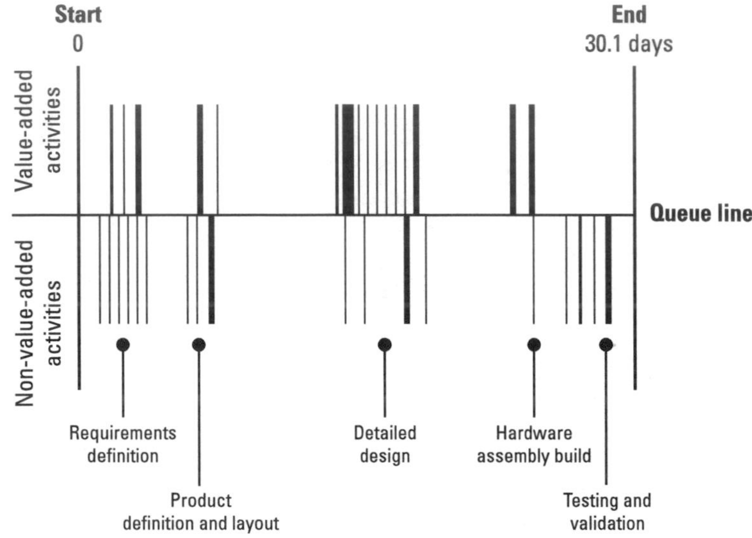

Figure 3-4. Time-Value Map for Developing Switches

TYPICAL PROBLEMS IN PRODUCT DEVELOPMENT

Let's now explore some additional issues that affect the product development process. The intent is to highlight problems—common in many companies—associated with product development, and to provide a perspective of the opportunities for improvement by applying lean principles.

Problem #1: Multitasking

Regarding the concept of flow, a problem facing many companies is the issue of multitasking. *Multitasking* is the concept associated with employees working multiple jobs concurrently. It can lead to the creation of bottlenecks that impede the movement of work quickly through the value stream. On the human side, multitasking can lead to inefficiency and a higher incidence of mistakes.

Experience gained from working with many companies has demonstrated that efficiency increases when an employee works a second job to fill in dead time that may exist with the person's primary task. Beyond two jobs, however, multitasking becomes problematic because the employee repeatedly needs to start and stop additional projects, which creates waste and leads to inefficiency. This condition is magnified as the employee undertakes more and more jobs. Consequently, the goal of every organization should be to minimize the effects of multitasking. This will enable employees to become more efficient, reduce cycle time, and maximize value-added work.

Another issue that can have an impact on flow that is linked to the concept of multitasking is the condition of an employee's workstation. Figure 3-5 shows an example of a workstation in disarray. A cluttered workstation is not necessarily a problem in itself; rather, it can be an indicator of potential problems related to flow and multitasking.

Figure 3-5. Employee Workstation

By observing a workstation like this, several questions come to mind:

- How well is this employee managing his or her work?
- Does the employee know all of the tasks he/she has in his or her work queue?

- Could this employee's activities be a bottleneck in the process?
- Is this employee overloaded with work?
- Does this employee have an issue with multitasking?

Once again, this may be an area of consideration and an opportunity for improvement related to flow. Incidentally, implementation of the 5S program (described in Chapter 2) is an excellent way to improve the condition of employee workstations and begin the organization's lean transformation.

Problem #2: Workload Exceeding the Company's Resource Capacity

Due to the intense pressures to reduce costs, another problem many companies face in today's business environment attempting to do-more-with-less, is the issue of resource and workload management. As shown in Figure 3-6, many companies associated with product development operate in an environment depicted by the graphic on the left. As you can see, there is a great disparity between the resource capacity in the product development organization and the amount of work that needs to be done. Over time, this issue worsens and is compounded due to the introduction of unplanned work and new opportunities. As you can imagine, the adverse effect of this condition on a company is substantial in terms of inefficiencies associated with employee multitasking, bottlenecking, and missed schedules and commitments.

The goal for companies in the area of resource and workload management is to achieve the condition depicted by the graphic on the right, where the effective resource capacity is matched to the actual work to be completed, or, in other words, where demand matches capacity. Also notice that the ultimate goal here is to build in a buffer for the resource capacity that enables the company to take on some additional, unplanned work that almost assuredly will show up and need to be completed.

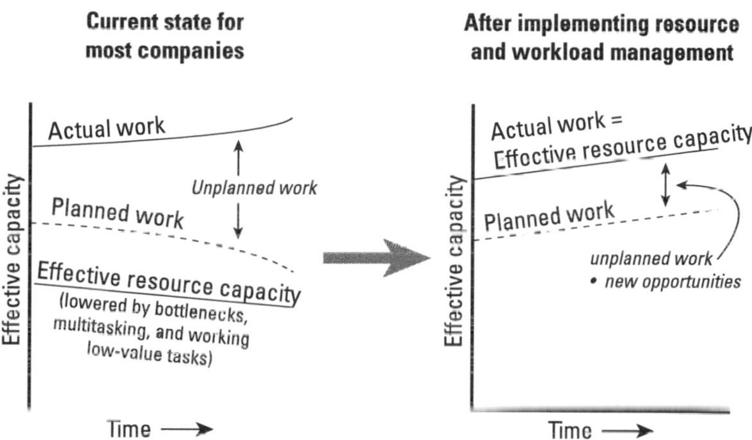

Figure 3-6. Resource and Workload Management

In today's environment, companies are increasingly looking to create and manage their resource pool through a practice known as globalization, or what is recognized by the more commonly used term as outsourcing. Companies typically pursue outsourcing for economic reasons or as an avenue to increase the company's effective resource capacity. Regardless of the merits of the strategy, companies that undertake this approach need to manage outsourced work and resources in the same manner as their internal resources.

Problem #3: Managing Customer and Technical Requirements

Many companies launch projects with established completion dates and milestones before they have the project requirements completely locked down. Consequently, another major issue for companies involved with product development is in the area of managing customer and technical requirements.

As the project evolves through the development process, the company is required to initiate the detailed design phase to ensure it meets the project schedule and to also ensure it has

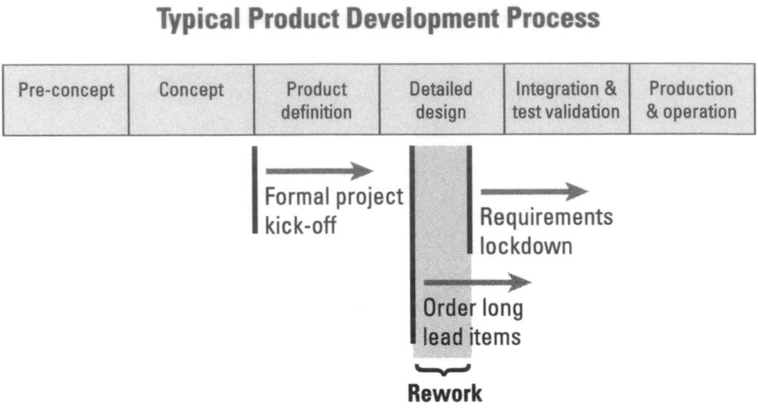

Typical Product Development Process

Pre-concept	Concept	Product definition	Detailed design	Integration & test validation	Production & operation

Formal project kick-off

Requirements lockdown

Order long lead items

Rework

Figure 3-7. Managing Customer and Technical Requirements

time to manufacture and procure long leadtime items[1] (see Figure 3-7). However, in situations where the requirements are still not locked down by this time, the company has to make assumptions concerning the requirements, and it therefore assumes a high degree of risk. This often leads to excessive amounts of rework, due to changing requirements after the company's assumptions were made and work was initiated.

There are two possible ways to address this issue. One way is to manage project requirements and delay the initiation of the downstream steps in the process until the requirements are locked down. The second way is to reduce the cycle time and improve the efficiency in the downstream processes, thereby affording additional time for the requirements to be locked down.

Additional Problems

The process of developing products is complex and influenced by many factors. Consequently, companies eager to improve

1. For software development, procurement of long leadtime items is not an issue. However, a viable method for this industry, as well as other industries of information products, is to manage project and customer requirements through focus groups supported by alpha/beta testing.

their product development process are faced with many issues. Multitasking, workload exceeding resource capacity, and managing customer and technical requirements are key issues that need to be addressed. But there are additional issues that companies encounter and have to deal with in order to make improvements in product development. These issues can be summarized into the following four basic categories:

Process Management and Control

Common problems in this category include:

- Lack of visual performance and scheduling controls in the office area
- Cluttered and disorganized work areas
- Priorities that are based on hot lists and voice mails
- Metrics that do not measure process outputs or desired behaviors

People

Issues in this category include:

- High degrees of expediting and special coordination
- Erosion of the company's technical and experience base
- People-based versus process-based activities
- High levels of multitasking and personnel turnover
- Issues with personnel working on common tasks that are not co-located or electronically linked through their workstations and software systems

Process Attributes

Problems in this area include:

- Process steps where queue times are prevalent, communication is poor, and empowerment is limited
- Projects that are launched with an unclear problem statement (or none at all)

- Projects that lack definition
- No project linkage between supplier and manufacturing process and capability

Support Systems

Problems in this category include:

- Unorganized or incomplete databases related to product information and knowledge that is needed for new product design
- Lack of clarity in the continuous improvement process
- Disconnects in product strategy and knowledge between the marketing and product development organizations

Identifying Product Development Problems in Your Company

Let's conclude this topic by asking you to consider the material presented thus far in this chapter and relate the issues presented to your own process. Consider the following questions:

1. Does your product development process have any of these wastes?
2. If so, what is the impact to your business?
3. Do you currently measure these wastes?
4. And finally, do you have an improvement strategy to address these issues?

Hopefully, the information presented in this chapter will enable you to start viewing your processes from a new perspective.

THE LEGEND OF THE GOLDEN PROJECT

Have you ever worked on an exceptionally rewarding project or program in your past that accomplished some amazing results? Typically, these projects are the highlight of one's career. Hopefully, you've had the pleasure of working on one of these projects. If you have, consider the characteristics of the project that made the effort so exceptional:

- Were the objectives clear and urgent?
- Were the participants capable and committed?
- Was there a concentrated effort to complete the project on time?

Chances are the answer is "yes" to all of these questions. Projects of this type are what I like to refer to as golden projects.

Unfortunately, golden projects have historically not occurred very often. But consider the following question: Were the characteristics that made the golden project so successful similar to the lean concepts and principles that were introduced in Chapter 2?

GUIDING PRINCIPLES FOR PRODUCT DEVELOPMENT

Before we begin our discussion of lean implementation in product development in Part Two of this book, let's go back to the five lean principles discussed earlier that essentially summarize the overall lean philosophy. Regarding product development, three additional guiding principles are presented that are instrumental in the successful implementation of lean concepts in the area of product development. The three guiding principles are:

1. Work on what's important.
2. Concentrate the work.
3. Reuse knowledge.

These guiding principles are not intended to replace the five traditional lean principles (listed in Chapter 2); instead, these three principles represent an extension of the existing principles geared towards the needs of the product development process (as depicted in Figure 3-8). They are intended to be high-level guideposts for developing an improvement strategy. Let's take a look at each one in more detail.

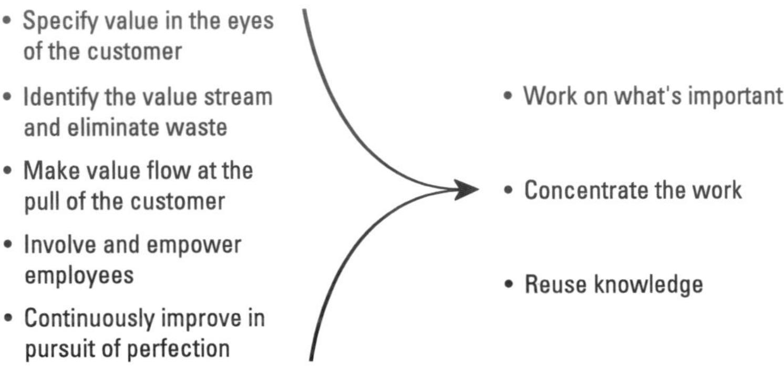

Figure 3-8. Guiding Principles for Product Development

Work on What's Important

Work on what's important means to pick the right projects and generate flow. Pick projects with high business value that align with the core competencies of the business. In addition, establish clear requirements in terms of true customer needs and determine how these requirements align with the company's known technologies and process capabilities. Identify any gaps that may exist.

Concentrate the Work

Concentrate the work means to minimize multitasking and match work demand to resource capacity. It also deals with human resource issues that relate to staffing projects appropriately with required and capable resources, as well as facilitating communication and teamwork through physical co-location or virtual workstation hook-ups linked through electronic mediums.

Reuse Knowledge

Reuse knowledge means to leverage the company's existing product portfolio, product knowledge, and technical skill base in support of new product design. Use appropriate levels of expertise, learn as much as you can, and capture the knowledge you have. Use project management disciplines to make the process repeatable, develop standard processes when possible, and minimize hand-offs and process interruption.

Understanding problems in the product development process from the perspective of lean principles is quite revealing. Armed with this information, we are now ready to move on to Part Two of this book and launch lean product development.

PART TWO

Launching Lean Product Development

Part Two describes how to assess the current state of the product development process and introduces a methodology for developing an improvement plan. A case study provides additional insight into following these approaches.

CHAPTER 4

Conducting a Baseline Assessment

So how do we begin our journey of initiating improvements related to the product development process? To understand what improvements need to be made, it is important to first understand the current state of the process. Understanding the current state represents the starting point, or the baseline, for initiating improvement. Consequently, the first step in the improvement of the product development process is to conduct an assessment, or what is more commonly referred to as a baseline event.

A *baseline event* represents the best opportunity to gain a thorough understanding of the current environment. Specifically, a baseline assessment:

- Identifies where problems exist
- Shapes a vision for the future
- Determines where to start and what to do
- Obtains management commitment to proceed with an improvement plan

The scope of baseline events can vary greatly. In general, events can be conducted at a business unit level, product line level, functional department level, or process level. A successful baseline event requires some planning and up-front data gathering, the commitment of a cross-functional assessment team chartered by management, and facilitation by knowledgeable individuals with experience in conducting baseline events.

GETTING STARTED

Baseline events can be orchestrated by using several different formats to achieve the desired results. However, there are some basic steps that should be taken before the actual event begins, regardless of the format that is used to ensure success:

Step 1: Ensure that the Business Unit or Department Will Support the Baseline Process

A baseline event is a significant undertaking for an organization. Consequently, the first prerequisite is to ensure that the organization is committed to supporting the baseline process and implementing the recommendations that will result from the effort.

Step 2: Select Individuals for the Baseline Assessment Core Team

The baseline assessment core team is a group of individuals selected by the organization to conduct the baseline event. The size of the team will depend on the scope of the baseline to be conducted. In addition, individuals should be selected who are open-minded and willing to explore new ideas. Finally, individuals should be identified who may not be part of the core team, but who might be required on an as-needed basis during the course to the baseline event.

Step 3: Include Management Input in Selecting the Baseline Event Date

Consideration should be given to ensuring that other significant business or company events do not conflict with the baseline event date. Also, consideration should be given to the schedules and availability of key personnel and management representatives who need to participate in baseline debriefings during the course of the event.

Step 4: Determine and Collect Up-front Data Prior to the Baseline Event

During this step, identify and collect data that will be needed to support the baseline event. Therefore, identify who is responsible for obtaining the data, and then determining when it is required and where it should be sent. (Regarding the destination, it is recommended that a focal point is selected to receive all data, follow-up, and to ensure timely responses are received prior to the event.) In addition, allow adequate time to analyze the data and generate results.

Step 5: Distribute Customer Surveys (If Required)

Depending on the nature of the baseline assessment, the baseline assessment core team may decide to distribute surveys as a way to obtain additional data in support of the baseline event. If this step is taken, allow adequate time for the respondents to complete the survey. Also, coordinate the timing of this activity with the selection of the baseline event dates.

Step 6: Communicate with the Management Team

It is imperative that the management team understands its role in supporting the baseline event. This includes attendance of daily debriefings during the baseline event as well as overall support of the process, particularly with regard to supporting the vision and business transformation to the future state.

Step 7: Prepare the Baseline Core Team

Conduct training for the core team members in terms of roles and responsibilities regarding the baseline event process. Training should include an overview of a lean business enterprise with emphasis on the seven types of waste (discussed in Chapters 2 and 3—see Figures 2-5 and 3-2).

CONDUCTING A BASELINE EVENT

As previously stated, the structure of a baseline event can take on many forms and is influenced by a number of factors including:

- The scope of the event
- The complexity and size of the hosting organization
- Knowledge of issues and problems associated with the current state

Experience has shown that diligence and up-front planning regarding the preparation phase of the baseline event yields better chances for success. Although baseline event formats can vary, they all contain the same fundamental elements. Figure 4-1 provides an example of a popular format that contains these elements.

As you can see in Figure 4-1, the actual event is laid out in five blocks, plus time required for the pre-work. The size and complexity of each organization will influence the duration of the event, which is typically no more than a few days. For example, in large and complex companies with product development organizations representing hundreds of individuals, baseline events can take up to a week to perform. Once again, this is a proposed format that can be tailored to suit a particular organization. Regarding this particular format, let's examine some of the key elements in more detail.

The Discovery Team's Tour and First Impressions Assessment

Armed with information and data from the pre-baseline activities, one of the initial actions of the baseline core team to kick off the event is to conduct a tour of the business area under review. In other words, the team walks through every operating aspect of the process under examination. Depending on the process, the core team may elect to remain as one team or break down into smaller teams to address different aspects of the

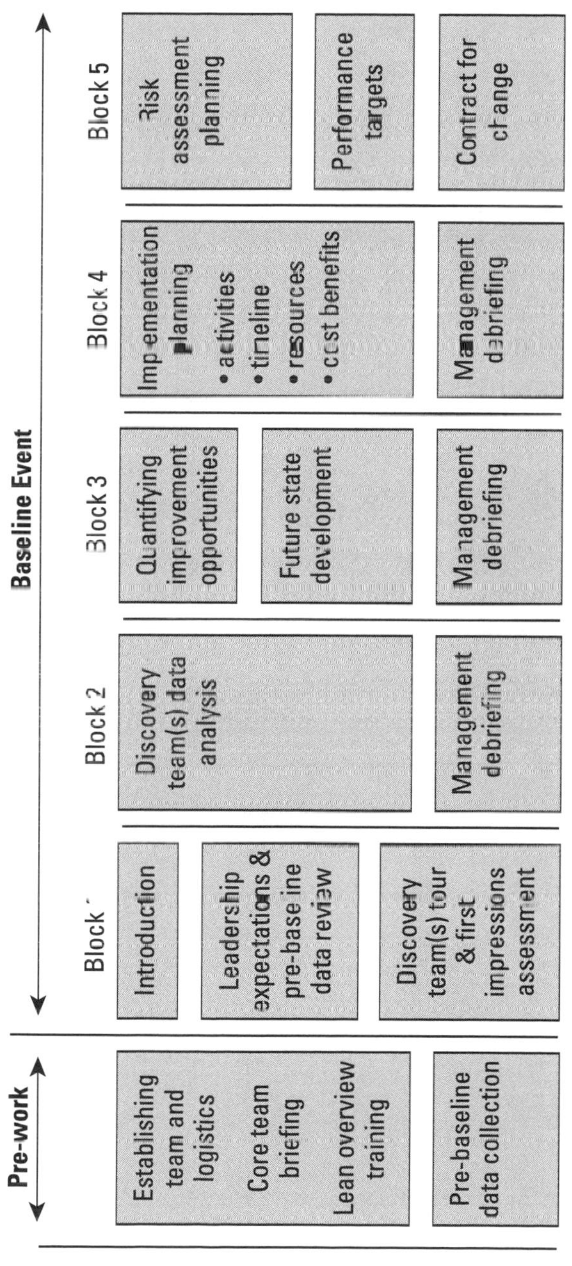

Figure 4-1. Format for Conducting a Baseline Event

overall process. By the very nature of this task, because teams are in a learning mode and discovering new information during the phase of the baseline event, the teams are appropriately called discovery teams.

The discovery team members are chartered with the responsibility of noting their first impressions during the tour and documenting what they observe as undesirable effects (UDEs). A UDE is an observed difference between the current state and the general vision of a lean enterprise. It is important that discovery team members be observant and look for clues to potential problems.

For example, some clues could be outdated metrics, work-flow choke points and bottlenecks, housekeeping issues related to disorderly work areas and poor cleanliness, and out-of-date schedules. In addition, discovery teams are encouraged to ask questions of employees who are working hands-on in the areas under review. Some sample questions include:

- What is the top thing that keeps you from making your goals every day?
- How often do you encounter problems in making your goals?
- What communication takes place between you and your team?
- How many jobs are you assigned to work on?
- How do you know what to work on next?
- If there is a conflict in work priorities, how is it resolved?
- How often do you have equipment problems, and how long is the equipment typically under repair?
- Where do you go to get information required for you do to your job?

During the course of asking questions, it is important for team members to be friendly and open, and they should thank participants for their time and support.

Discovery teams have the freedom to focus on any aspect of the process under review. However, regarding product development, as a result of conducting numerous baseline events, history has shown that discovery teams habitually gravitate towards five primary problem areas. As a result, it is suggested that the discovery teams be structured and focused on these five key areas. Experience has demonstrated this approach to be extremely successful. These five teams are as follows:

Team 1: Focusing on Product Development Demand and Workload

This team is chartered with assessing the incoming workload demands compared to the company's goals, capacity, and capabilities. In addition, this team is chartered with assessing the current work allocation process and identifying workload issues associated with multitasking, bottlenecks, rework, and expediting.

Team 2: Focusing on Customer Value and Requirements Flow-Down

This team is chartered with assessing whether critical customer and management requirements are adequately identified and communicated throughout the product development organization. This assessment includes an evaluation of the effectiveness of the product development process in meeting customer requirements.

Team 3: Focusing on Parts Standardization and Operations Integration

This team is chartered with determining the reuse level of product best practices in new product development. In addition, this team assesses the impact of new parts in the manufacturing and operations environment, material modernization and parts standardization opportunities, and design for manufacture (DFM) and technology issues.

Team 4: Focusing on the Blueprint Drawing Revision Process and Causes of Software Defects

This team is chartered with assessing blueprint drawing revisions and software defects identified by the company. The quantity of drawing revisions processed by the company is typically a good indicator of the overall effectiveness and health of the product development process. For example, this assesses whether the company processes a large number of engineering modifications during the production phase to fix problems that could have been resolved during the development phase of the product. Consequently, this team reviews the volume of revisions requested, the reasons for the requests, and the effectiveness of the process in processing and implementing the requests.

Similarly, software defects are also a good indicator in assessing the state of the software development process. By understanding the issues that cause defects, improvements can be made that eliminate these issues and result in a more robust development process.

Team 5: Focusing on the Product Development Postmortem

This team is chartered with identifying the current performance of the product development process. To determine this, the team examines two or three representative projects and reviews the end-to-end results of the projects in terms of the product's performance, marketing issues, staffing, process adherence, and schedule and budget issues to assess root causes for overall project success or failure.

The Discovery Team Analysis

With the data gathering effort complete, the next step is to analyze the data. Specifically, the goal of this step is to understand where real value is delivered in the process. In addition, this step identifies the major areas of waste and the root causes for that waste. The creation of value stream maps help analyze these issues. Also, the team members consolidate the UDEs they've acquired and assess them to determine the cause-and-effects relationships.

Several tools can be used to help the discovery teams analyze data, including process maps, relationship diagrams, nominal group techniques, prioritization matrices, and others.

Quantifying Improvement Opportunities

A key step in the baseline event is the transition from the data gathering, problem identification, and analysis tasks to developing plans for improvement. Consequently, it is imperative for the core team to clarify and prioritize the improvement opportunities before starting the planning process. Some of the key elements include:

- Identifying the major areas of waste
- Estimating the level of waste (in dollars)
- Estimating the total improvement opportunity (in dollars)

Future State Development

The deliverable of the future state development activity is a vision of the future for the company that maximizes customer value. This includes establishing goals and performance measures.

Management's role is critical in supporting the future state development activity. The company's leaders have the best overall view of what is required to be successful in the marketplace, and they can provide perspective on establishing realistic and achievable goals. Establishing goals that are too low will produce minimal benefits; establishing excessively high goals necessitates additional resources and time, and it increases the risk of the effort stalling before it can be completed. Consequently, establishing appropriate goals requires continual questioning of the trade-off of the business value of the activity versus the investment.

Implementation Planning

This activity deals with establishing a high-level plan and identifying specific projects for achieving the future state. The plan includes identifying and sequencing the major work activities, establishing an implementation timeline, and estimating the resource requirements and identifying critical skill-set needs.

A key factor that supports the implementation planning is a cost-benefits analysis of each project. The management team should review this analysis to obtain agreement that the projected benefit from each project justifies the investment. Due to time constraints during the baseline event, a more detailed project plan will most likely need to be developed at some point after the event.

Finally, it is necessary to define a project management infrastructure for the overall implementation plan. To facilitate this, a team is formed and chartered with carrying out the implementation plan. This team is responsible for determining the level of project management, as well as logistics for team meetings and management reviews related to frequency, required attendance, format for agendas, and so on.

Risk Assessment Planning

In conjunction with developing the implementation plan, it is necessary to perform a risk assessment in order to understand the issues related to achieving the future state goals. The risk assessment includes identifying and ranking implementation risks, identifying actions to mitigate the risk, and ranking their expected effectiveness.

The risk assessment will also include an assessment of the project goals. The assessment should attempt to answer the following questions:

- Are the goals clear?
- How will they be measured?
- Are the metrics tied to the business success?

Performance Targets

To ensure the success of the project, a clear set of in-process performance targets should be identified from the implementation plan. These performance targets include identifying specific goals and completion dates. Key metrics that monitor progress towards attaining the goals are also established. The performance targets should be documented and presented to the management team for agreement. This step is a precursor to the *Contract for Change*.

The Contract for Change

The Contract for Change is a formal agreement signed between the implementation team and management. The agreement is intended to be a binding contract between both parties. Figure 4-2 shows a portion of a Contract for Change. By signing the Contract for Change, the management team agrees to:

- Establish and communicate the future state vision
- Provide the required human and financial resources
- Advocate the transformation process and work cooperatively to remove barriers

By signing the Contract for Change, the implementation team agrees to:

- Advocate and promote the future state vision
- Achieve the goals of the implementation plan within the allocated budget and on-schedule

Contract for Change

This document is a *Contract for Change* for the Product Development and Site Leadership Teams and concerns the implementation of a Six Sigma Lean Enterprise. The baseline assessment process is a data-driven approach to gain an understanding of the current state and determine the sequence of initial improvement activities. Product design and development is a key process to the financial and customer satisfaction performance of our business enterprise. The onset of this journey represents a significant investment in the future and will provide a solid foundation for growth and productivity through greater employee and customer satisfaction.

The notion of a *Lean Enterprise* includes manufacturing, engineering, and all administrative and support activities of our business. Work and process standardization, small-lot and single-piece flow, mistake-proofing, cycle time reduction, and structuring the business to meet customer demand are key elements of the Lean Enterprise. It must be clear that these thoughts apply to every business, engineering, and manufacturing process within our company.

Implementing a Lean Enterprise is not easy. Significant organizational, structural, and skill changes will be part of our successful journey. There will be long-term positive business improvements including:

- TBD percent productivity increase
- TBD percent reduction in engineering effort and product development cycle lead-time
- TBD percent product cost reduction
- TBD percent product quality level increase

By signing the Contract for Change, the Site and Product Development Leadership agree to:

- Support, refine, and implement the Product Development Lean Enterprise plan by:
  - Providing the required financial and human resources on a timely basis
  - Advocating the transformation process and working cooperatively to remove barriers

Figure 4-2. Example of a Contract for Change

CONDUCTING FOLLOW-UP BASELINE ASSESSMENTS FOR CONTINUOUS IMPROVEMENT

As a company embarks on a path of continuous improvement, it is logical to ask how often additional baseline events should be conducted to support the improvement activity. Based on experience conducting numerous baseline events, it is recommended that follow-up baseline events be administered in two- to three-year time periods.

As a company continues to make advances in the product development process, it is important to periodically assess the effectiveness of each improvement activity. The follow-up baseline events help answer these questions regarding the company's overall improvement strategy:

- How effective are the improvement activities that have been implemented to date?
- Do the same issues identified in the original baseline event still exist today?
- Have new issues emerged that need to be addressed?

By answering these questions through subsequent baseline events, a company will be able to validate or modify the improvement plan accordingly. Typically, compared to the original baseline effort, the follow-up events are streamlined versions. By leveraging and updating much of the data from the original event, a company can complete these subsequent events in less time.

To help establish improvement plans for product development throughout the baseline activity, a maturity path assessment has been developed, as shown in Figure 4-3 beginning on page 61. This five-phased assessment, structured in a checklist format, outlines key items to be implemented as a company undertakes the challenge of improving its product development process. By updating and maintaining the maturity path assessment as a living document, the company can identify items that are completed and new opportunities to address.

A baseline assessment represents a comprehensive approach to truly understanding process issues. Based on its importance as the starting point for improvement, Chapter 5 offers a case study to provide additional clarity in conducting an assessment.

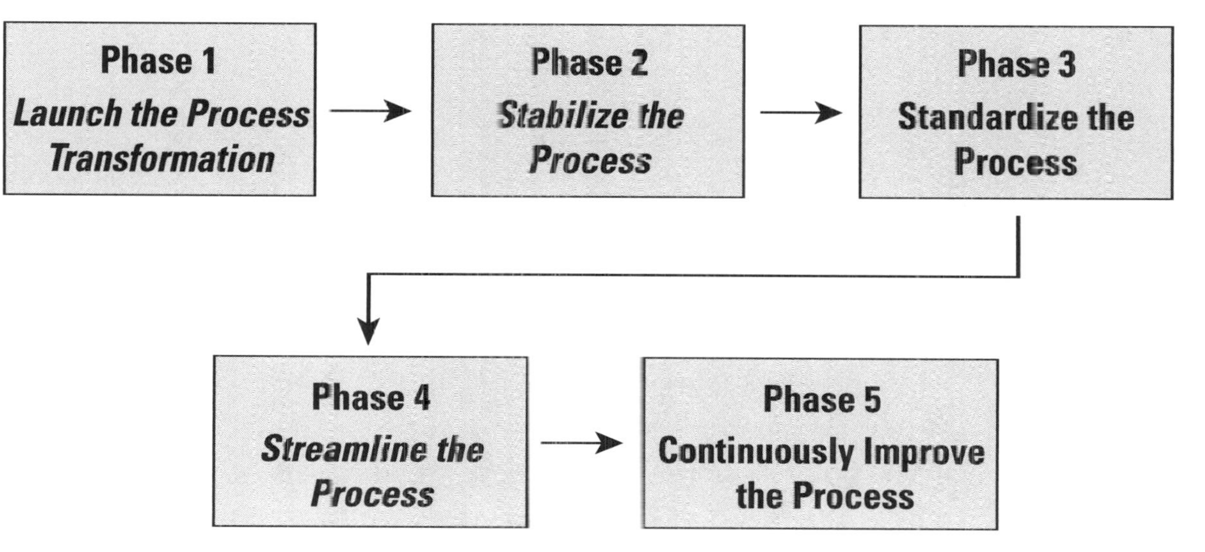

Figure 4-3. Product Development Maturity Path

Figure 4-3. Product Development Maturity Path (continued)

Phase 1

Launch the Process Transformation

Purpose:

☑ *Get leadership buy-in*

☑ *Develop a plan*

☑ *Resource the plan*

- ☐ Provide lean overview training for leadership team
- ☐ Train engineering leadership team
- ☐ Establish improvement expectations
- ☐ Select dedicated leader
- ☐ Develop improvement measures
- ☐ Conduct product development baseline event
- ☐ Identify product development critical path and value stream
- ☐ Determine and communicate process improvement vision
- ☐ Review engineering blueprint revision—process performance and drivers
- ☐ Establish and resource sequenced plan to create project and information flow
- ☐ Align product development strategy to the market (cycle time, cost, and quality improvements)
- ☐ Align implementation plan to business strategic and operating plan

Source: C. Fiore, *Lean Strategies for Product Development*, ASQ, 2003

Figure 4-3. Product Development Maturity Path (continued)

Phase 2

→ ***Stabilize the Process***

Purpose:

- ☑ *Stabilize the process*
- ☑ *Focus the resources*
- ☑ *Align the culture*

- ☐ Communicate baseline results and initial plan
- ☐ Identify standard process tasks
- ☐ Establish reuse policy and procedures for commodity-type parts
- ☐ Determine product and part families
- ☐ Implement procedures for engineering blueprint revision process stabilization
- ☐ Implement process quality measurement
- ☐ Implement design process measurements and visual controls
- ☐ Minimize identified bottlenecks
- ☐ Evaluate and manage work-in-process to generate flow
- ☐ Initiate 5-S (sort, stabilize, shine, standardize, and sustain) implementation
- ☐ Provide new part impact training
- ☐ Focus critical skills and processes to minimize multitasking and changeover
- ☐ Facilitate lean transformation integrated through goal development
- ☐ Institute program management within the product development process

Source: C. Fiore, *Lean Strategies for Product Development*, ASQ, 2003

Figure 4-3. Product Development Maturity Path (continued)

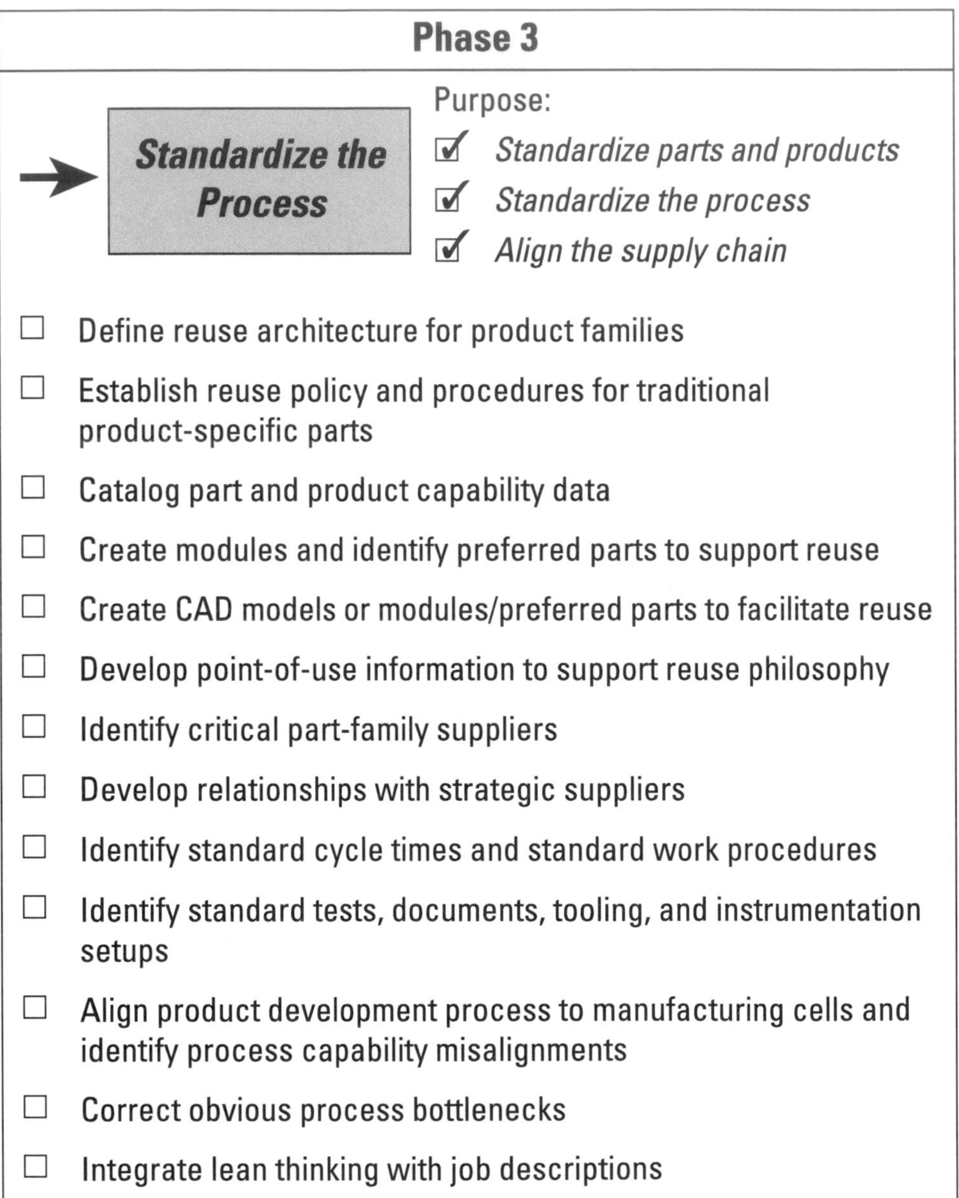

Phase 3

Standardize the Process

Purpose:

- ☑ *Standardize parts and products*
- ☑ *Standardize the process*
- ☑ *Align the supply chain*

- ☐ Define reuse architecture for product families
- ☐ Establish reuse policy and procedures for traditional product-specific parts
- ☐ Catalog part and product capability data
- ☐ Create modules and identify preferred parts to support reuse
- ☐ Create CAD models or modules/preferred parts to facilitate reuse
- ☐ Develop point-of-use information to support reuse philosophy
- ☐ Identify critical part-family suppliers
- ☐ Develop relationships with strategic suppliers
- ☐ Identify standard cycle times and standard work procedures
- ☐ Identify standard tests, documents, tooling, and instrumentation setups
- ☐ Align product development process to manufacturing cells and identify process capability misalignments
- ☐ Correct obvious process bottlenecks
- ☐ Integrate lean thinking with job descriptions

Source: C. Fiore, *Lean Strategies for Product Development*, ASQ, 2003

Figure 4-3. Product Development Maturity Path (continued)

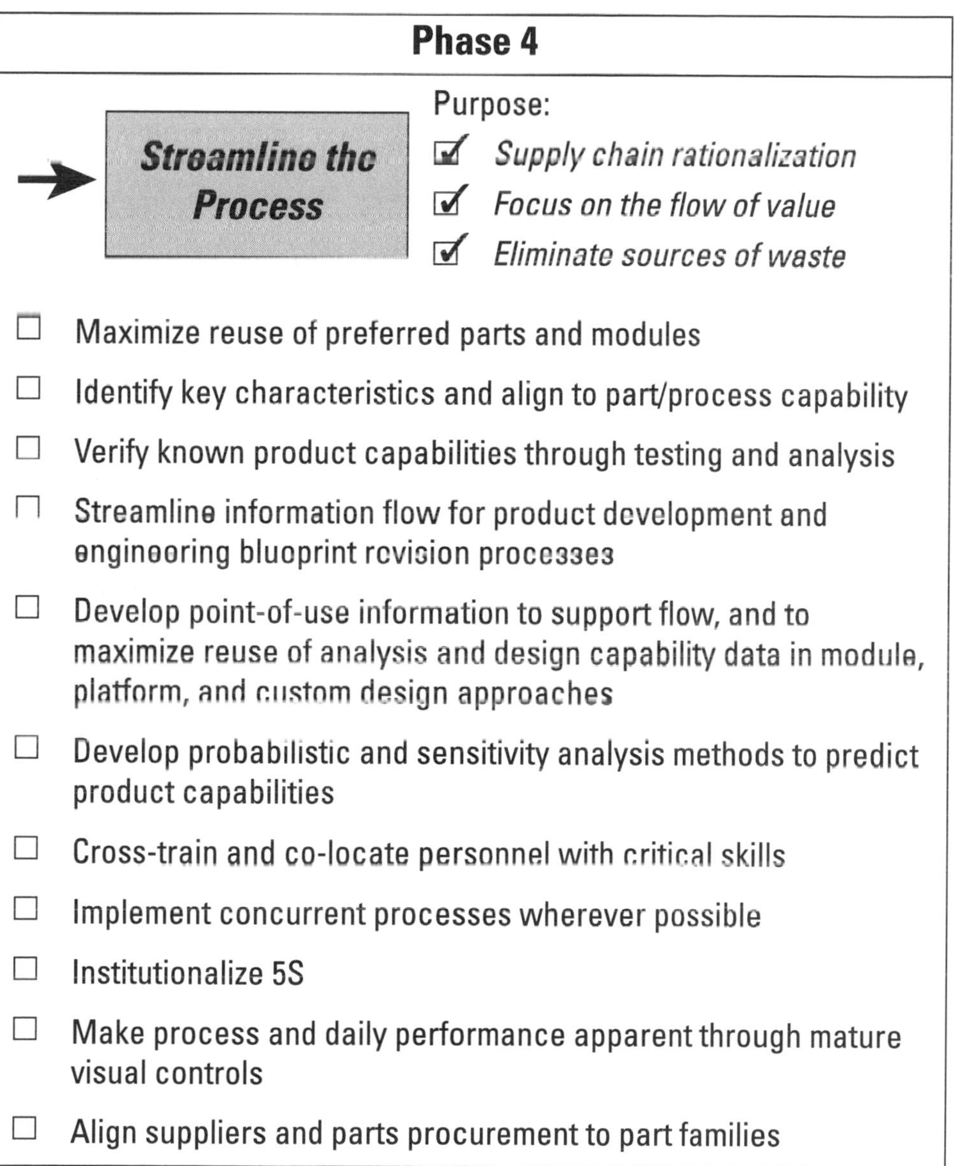

Source: C. Fiore, *Lean Strategies for Product Development*, ASQ, 2003

Figure 4-3. Product Development Maturity Path (continued)

Phase 5

→ ***Continuously Improve the Process***

Purpose:

☑ *Optimize the supply chain*

☑ *Mature the culture*

☑ *Design for a competitive advantage*

- ☐ Re-baseline product development process every 18 to 24 months
- ☐ Maintain improvement opportunities connected to business strategic and operating plan
- ☐ Redesign existing high-volume products to reduce cost and facilitate product flow in the factory
- ☐ Continue to improve information flow by automating design analysis and the selection of reuse components in product development tools
- ☐ Capture and utilize lessons learned; convert to best practices
- ☐ Connect design and product capability to business growth strategy
- ☐ Integrate customers and suppliers through the product development process via e-business
- ☐ Align processes with customer and market needs
- ☐ Maximize use of product development process as a competitive weapon
- ☐ Proactively extend product capabilities to meet market needs

Source: C. Fiore, *Lean Strategies for Product Development,* ASQ, 2003

CHAPTER 5

A Baseline Assessment Case Study

This chapter highlights the effectiveness of conducting a baseline assessment as the starting point for initiating process improvement by offering a case study about a fictitious company called Rotorworld. The data provided in this chapter do not include all information resulting from a baseline assessment. However, the case study does provide examples of team findings and a measure of insight into the approaches taken by discovery teams to acquire information that is used as the basis for triggering process improvement.

COMPANY BACKGROUND

The Rotorworld Company is a supplier of electric motors used in a variety of product applications, including small, home appliances, power tools, and lawn and garden equipment. For years, the company was recognized as a market leader in the manufacture of electric motors. Over the past year, however, Rotorworld has seen a dramatic drop-off in new business, and its leadership position in the marketplace has been slipping. A common theme heard from Rotorworld customers is that the company provides good and reliable products, but they cost too much and take too long to bring to market.

Rotorworld's leadership team realized a dramatic change needed to be made regarding its product development process. Unless the company could meet its customer needs in terms of lower-cost products and reduced cycle times, the continued viability of Rotorworld would be in doubt.

CREATING A PLATFORM FOR CHANGE

Rotorworld's leadership team realized it needed to react quickly. As a result of conducting a series of market analysis studies and hosting a series of discussions with customers and key Rotorworld managers, the company generated a list of expectations that it believed needed to be met, so that the company could regain customer confidence and restore its market position. These expectations are summarized in Figure 5-1.

Customer's Expectations

- Lower-cost products (20% reduction)
- Shorter time to market for products (50% reduction)
- Improvement in on-time delivery (15% improvement)

Rotorworld's Expections:

- Lower product development cost (30% reduction)
- Lower warranty costs (2X improvement)
- Improved program control (95% schedule adherence)

Figure 5-1. Rotorworld's Platform for Change

As you can see, Rotorworld outlined a series of very ambitious goals. The numbers represented a quantum leap in improvement over the company's existing level of performance.

As demonstrated by the quantified goals outlined in Figure 5-1, Rotorworld's leadership team took the first positive step towards instituting change in the organization. Management laid out expectations and goals that were well defined. By using numbers to help articulate goals, Rotorworld would be able to generate data and objective evidence to determine if its improvement activities met their expectations.

ROTORWORLD'S BASELINE ASSESSMENT

Rotorworld understood the purpose of a baseline assessment as the starting point for improvement, so it formed a core team to conduct such an assessment for the company's product development process. The core team comprised a cross section of individuals with varying degrees of involvement regarding the company's product development process. This involvement ranged from designers and engineers, who were intimately involved with the process on a daily basis, to procurement specialists who received engineering blueprint drawings and represented the internal customers of the process.

Rotorworld's baseline assessment event was planned to follow the format presented in Chapter 4. The core team conducted a series of meetings as a precursor to the actual event. In addition to completing the baseline prework, the team discussed the fundamental issues related to Rotorworld's product development process. Among the many issues discussed, team consensus believed that multitasking in the product development organization was a significant issue. To confirm this belief, the team elected to administer a survey prior to conducting the baseline event, to gain a better perspective of the magnitude of the problem. The data for the core team's survey is displayed in Figure 5-2.

The data indicated that each engineer was working on an average of four projects! These results confirmed the core team's suspicions concerning multitasking. The core team realized that this issue would need to be addressed further during the actual baseline event.

DISCOVERY TEAM DATA

The baseline event was convened with five discovery teams (suggested in Chapter 4) investigating the different elements of Rotorworld's product development process. Here are the findings and data generated from each team:

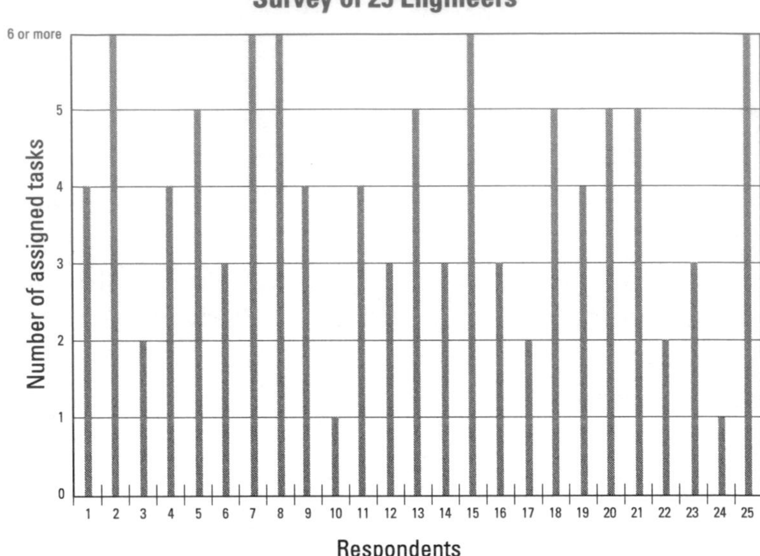

Figure 5-2. Rotorworld's Multitasking Survey Results

Team 1: Focusing on Product Development Demand and Workload

The team had already developed a good understanding of the multitasking issue as a result of the pre-baseline survey. As part of the baseline activity, the team reviewed data from Rotorworld's project management system and interviewed several project managers. Highlights of the team's findings included:

- No process for demand and capacity management
- Inadequate staffing during the initial stages of a project
- Very little dedication of resources to teams and a high degree of personnel changes
- Large backlog in design department: Data indicated the department was consistently overrunning budgets by 25 percent.

Team 2: Focusing on Customer Value and Requirements Flow-Down

This team reviewed project log books from a sampling of various completed projects. The intent of this activity was to assess the effectiveness of the product development process in meeting customer requirements. The team reviewed project data to understand how technical requirements were determined and addressed in terms of the product solution provided to the customer. A summary of the team's findings included:

- Projects were launched without a clear problem statement. Technical requirements were still evolving as the project was being worked, which resulted in rework.
- Product development process was not closely followed, and there was poor process discipline.
- Projects were not closed out, that is, administrative records and project phase gate data was not finalized and closed out when the projects were completed.

Team 3: Focusing on Parts Standardization and Operations Integration

Based on the characteristics of the products produced by Rotorworld, this team focused heavily on the opportunities related to product reuse. To accomplish this, the team reviewed five recently completed product designs. The team's findings found:

- Limited reuse of part designs in new applications (less than 10 percent of new products reused existing part designs)
- Poor infrastructure to support reuse strategy
- No linkage in matching supplier capability to part manufacturing requirements
- Lack of standards used in the product development process

Team 4: Focusing on the Blueprint Drawing Revision Process

The team reviewed drawing revision requests processed from the prior twelve months. In addition, the team created a value stream map to gain a perspective of value-added and non-value-added time associated with Rotorworld's process. In summary, the discovery team's finding concluded that:

- 92 percent of the revision requests were associated with fixing problems
- 95 percent of the total processing time was associated with performing non-value-added activities
- Practitioners in the process were not located near each other resulting in excessive transportation and other waste

Team 5: Focusing on the Product Development Postmortem

This team conducted an analysis of five recently completed projects. The results are shown in Figure 5-3. As you can see, the five projects that were evaluated did not score well relative to general customer criteria regarding performance, reliability, and cost. Even though the evaluation was somewhat subjective, based on the discovery team's determination of what constituted successful, marginal, and unsuccessful, the results clearly validated the message Rotorworld heard from its customers regarding the company's current state.

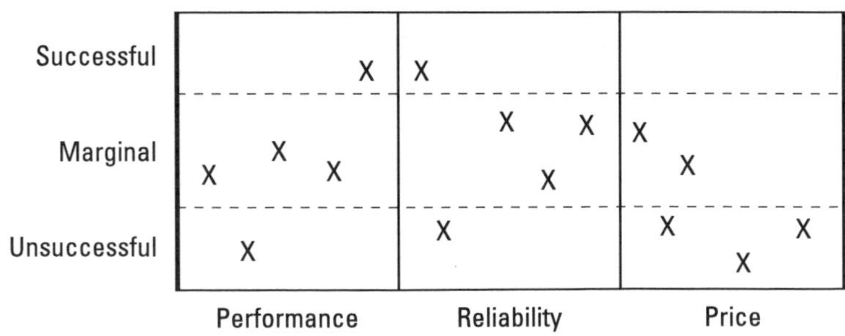

Figure 5-3. Rotorworld's Project Evaluation Results

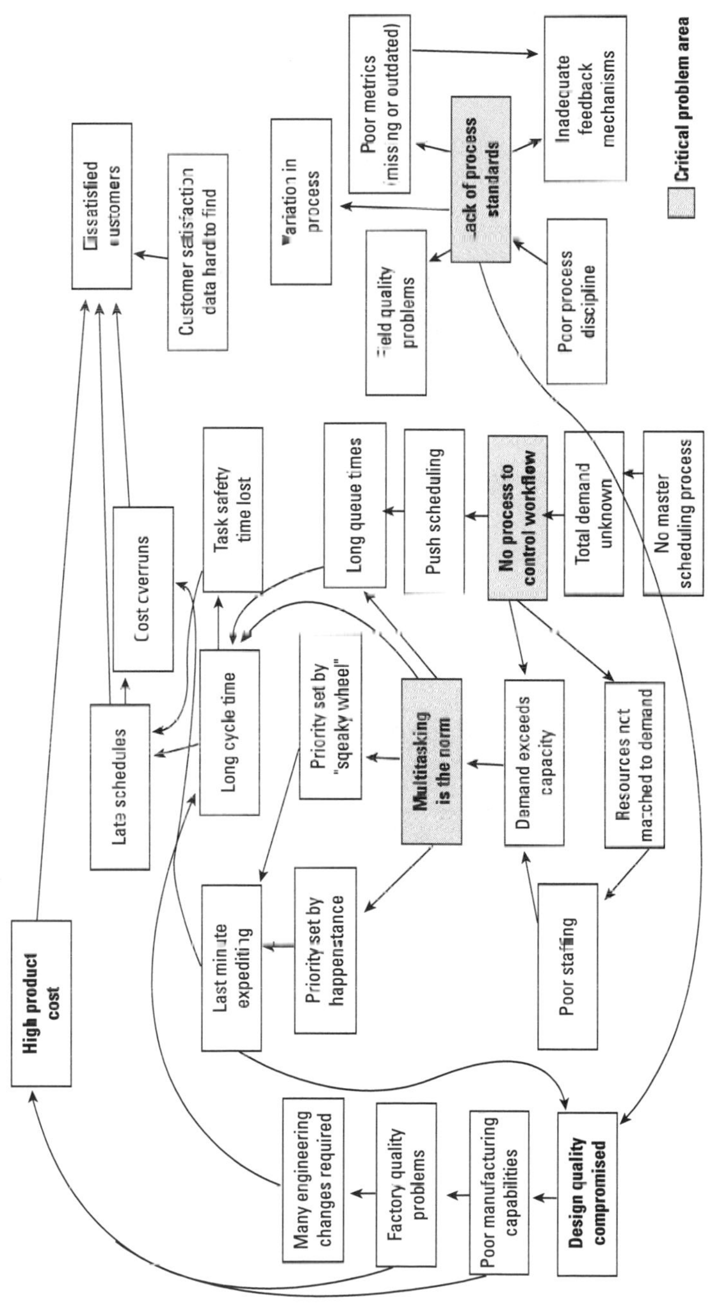

Figure 5-4. Linkage of Discovery Team UDEs

THE DISCOVERY TEAM'S ANALYSIS

The discovery teams convened to collectively review the UDEs generated by each team. This analysis included an activity to understand the linkage and relationships of the various issues identified by the teams for Rotorworld's process. The result of this activity is shown in Figure 5-4 (previous page). As you can see, the team identified multitasking, no workflow control, and a lack of standards as fundamental issues associated with Rotorworld's process.

Another element of the discovery team's analysis focused on assessing the value-added and non-value-added time of a typical employee performing product development tasks. The result of this effort is illustrated with the pie chart in Figure 5-5.

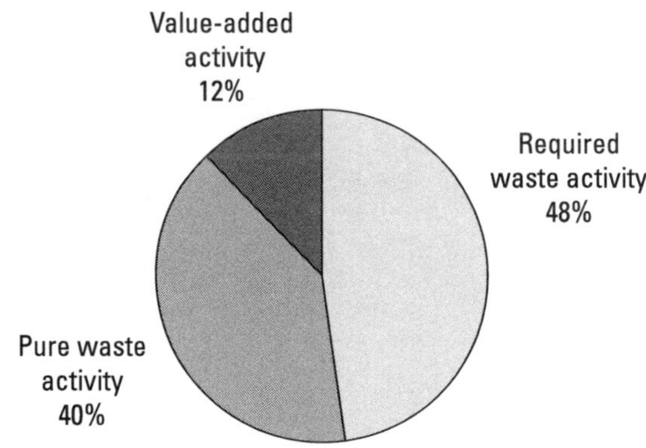

Figure 5-5. Breakdown of Work Tasks

The numbers are quite revealing. Employees devote only 12 percent of their time to activities that add value for the customer. Almost half of their time is associated with required waste activities, that is, tasks that need to be completed based on a company or customer requirement, but do not meet the three criteria for a value-added task. And 40 percent of the time was associated with purely non-value-added tasks, representing a significant opportunity for waste elimination.

BUILDING THE HOUSE OF PRODUCT DEVELOPMENT

Improving the product development process touches on a number of different activities. Similar to building a house in a logical sequence, experience has demonstrated that the benefits resulting from the implementation of the various product development activities are maximized when they follow a specific order. Consequently, the remainder of this book presents material in the recommended sequence of implementation for the product development process. Each chapter builds on elements of the prior one to create the house of product development, shown in Figure 5-6.

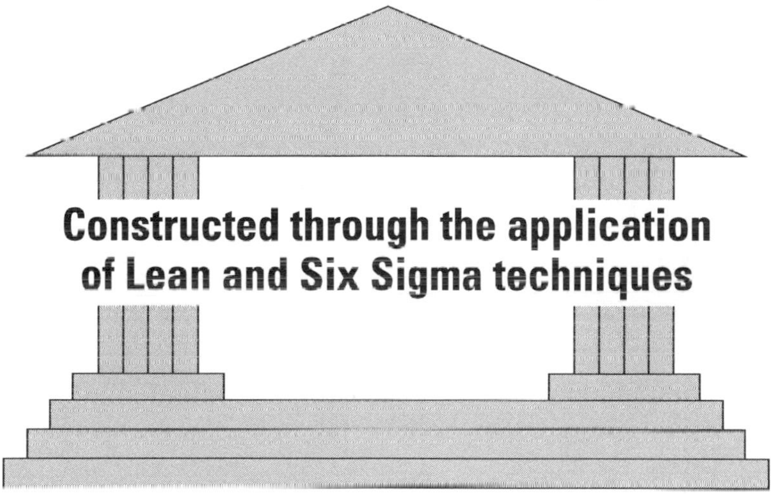

Figure 5-6. The House of Product Development

Chapter 6, in Part Three, begins this process by focusing on the relationship of matching a company's available resources to its workload for optimum efficiency, effectiveness, and productivity.

PART THREE

Stabilizing the Product Development Process

Part Three addresses fundamental elements needed for improving the product development process, which include resource and workload management, implementing a reuse strategy, and building the infrastructure to enable process improvement.

CHAPTER 6

Resource and Workload Management

As workload demands fluctuate, a company has to flex available resources to meet changing demand. Years of company downsizing, however, have made it increasingly difficult for companies to adequately support fluctuations that represent high-peak demand periods. This is the case with many companies involved with product development. Compounding this situation, product development organizations have been attempting to concurrently satisfy the requirements of:

- Customers demanding shorter product development cycle times
- Management dictating the need for more product and after-market support
- Factories requiring additional support to resolve product related problems and cost reductions

Consequently, the ability of product development organizations to balance their resource and workload demands has become a major issue.

THE NEED FOR RESOURCE AND WORKLOAD MANAGEMENT

In terms of resource management, the challenge for organizations is to achieve high productivity from scarce resources. To accomplish this, companies must first have a fundamental understanding of all of the demands of its resources. Next, companies must be capable of allocating their resources to the highest value projects. To achieve these objectives, companies should use a process that facilitates clear alignment of resources with workload demands, and provides the capability of adjusting resources in a timely fashion. Undermining these objectives, however, are issues of inadequate staffing, people turnover, and multitasking, which companies must also address.

For the product development organization, the primary issue associated with workload management is to effectively manage the work demands, while achieving the goal of reducing product development cycle time and cost. Consequently, the product development organization must overcome several systemic problems in this area, including:

- Launching projects with incomplete problem statements
- Driving accountability in meeting project plans and schedules
- Integrating unplanned and unscheduled work

Organizations that manage resources and workload poorly typically deal with issues where workload levels and the processing capability of resources are not matched. When the incoming work level exceeds the process output level, a bottleneck emerges. Expressed another way, a *bottleneck* occurs when workload demand exceeds resource capacity, resulting in high levels of work-in-process (WIP) and stagnation in the value stream. There are many examples of bottlenecks in everyday life, such as rush-hour traffic and checkout lines at the supermarket.

The impact of a bottleneck on a process is significant. Typically, work piles up in front of the bottleneck and overall process output is only as fast as the bottleneck allows. Consequently, the downstream steps in the process are underutilized, resulting in increased cost and inefficiency. This condition

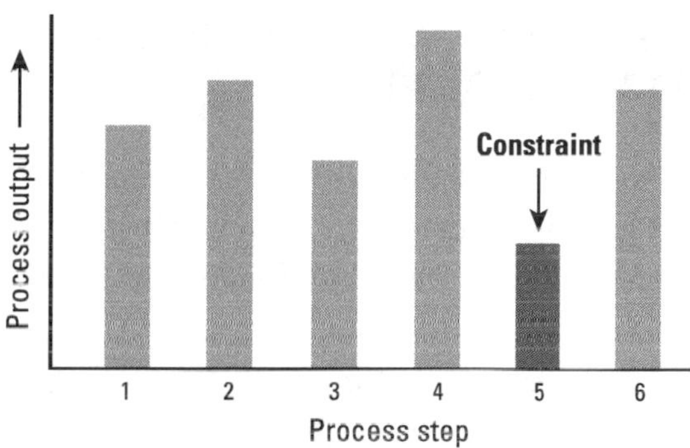

Figure 6-1. Process Exemplifying the Theory of Constraints

exemplifies the management philosophy known as the *theory of constraints*.

Simply stated, the theory of constraints contends that overall output of any process is limited, or constrained, by the least productive step in the process. For example, consider a process with six individual steps as depicted in Figure 6-1. As you can see, the output of each process step is on a relative scale, with process step 5 providing the lowest level of output. The theory of constraints states the overall output of this process is dictated by the output of process step 5. In other words, process step 5 is the constraint in this process. Improvements made to any other process step would not be beneficial until the output of process step 5 is increased to the point where the constraint is removed.

Poor resource and workload management is a major form of waste, and it increases product development cycle time. Data from companies indicate that resource and workload management issues reduce productivity and increase product development costs by more than 20 percent.

Clearly, resource and workload management represents a significant opportunity for improvement. If you recall the lean principles presented in Chapter 2, implementation of an effective resource and workload management process is a key step towards achieving flow.

STRATEGIES FOR IMPROVING RESOURCE AND WORKLOAD MANAGEMENT

There are several ways to address the issues of resource and workload management. The easiest way is simply to increase capacity by adding additional resources. Unfortunately, most companies do not have this luxury in light of the current business environment and continual cost pressures they face. Consequently, the only recourse for most companies is to improve the efficiency of the resources it already possesses. There are two general approaches to achieve this, as described in the following sections.

Increase the Effective Capacity of Existing Resources

There are three options that can be employed to increase the effective resource capacity. The first option is to eliminate waste and thereby minimize the effects of non-value-added tasks performed by workers—these associated with multitasking, expediting, and overloading. The second option is to shift resources and flex the organization's resource pool in response to process bottlenecks, absences, and so on. The third option for increasing the effective resource capacity is to make systemic improvements by improving tools, reducing variation, achieving higher levels of reuse, and increasing access to information.

Match Work Demand and Resource Capacity

There are two options that can be used to facilitate matching work demand to resource capacity. One option is to institute a process that insures new projects and work assignments are launched only when resources are available. This activity helps minimize the effects of multitasking and expediting. The second option is to establish a priority schedule for completing jobs in a work queue, with the goal of eliminating a process bottleneck and low-value work. For example, consider the work queue depicted in Figure 6-2.

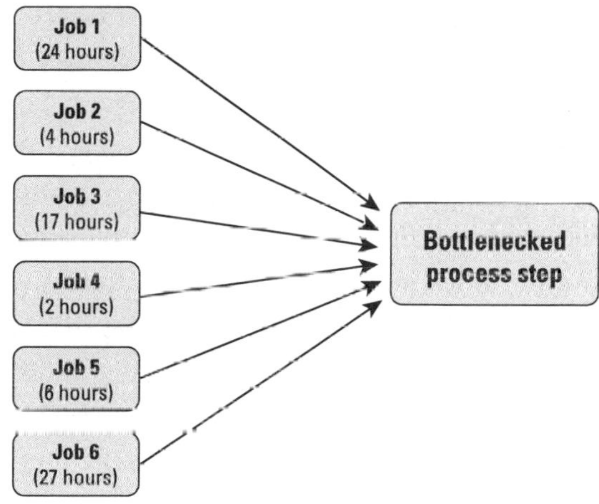

Figure 6-2. Managing a Work Queue

As you can see, Figure 6-2 depicts a work queue represented by six jobs for a bottlenecked process step. The hours contained within each box represent the estimated time to complete each job. The issue here is to achieve the proper balance in establishing a priority schedule for completing the six jobs, in order to alleviate the bottleneck, increase resource utilization, and maximize process output.

One option is to establish a sequence for completing jobs with priority given to ones that have minimal impact on the bottleneck. In other words, the jobs requiring the fewest hours to complete can be worked first. By doing this, the bottlenecked process step can generate output quicker and engage the downstream resources associated with the subsequent process steps in the shortest time possible. Consequently, referring to Figure 6-2, Job 4 could be worked first, followed by Jobs 2, 5, 3, 1, and 6, in that order.

In reality, any number of factors can create a bottleneck. However, the challenge for companies is to consider the key factors and adopt the appropriate strategy to manage the bottleneck and maximize output for the company.

In summary, the overall improvement strategy for resource and workload management is depicted in Figure 6-3. You may notice that the curve exhibits characteristics similar to an inverted Taguchi loss function curve. As Figure 6-3 illustrates, with a light workload and ample staffing, short cycle times can be achieved, but the costs are prohibitive. Conversely, an excessive workload results in large queues, bottlenecks, and high degrees of multitasking. Under this scenario, cycle times are long and costs are high, due to the inefficiencies in managing the work. The objective is to attain the right workload level in order to maximize workload efficiency—one that represents the best opportunity to achieve the cycle time and cost goals desired by the product development organization.

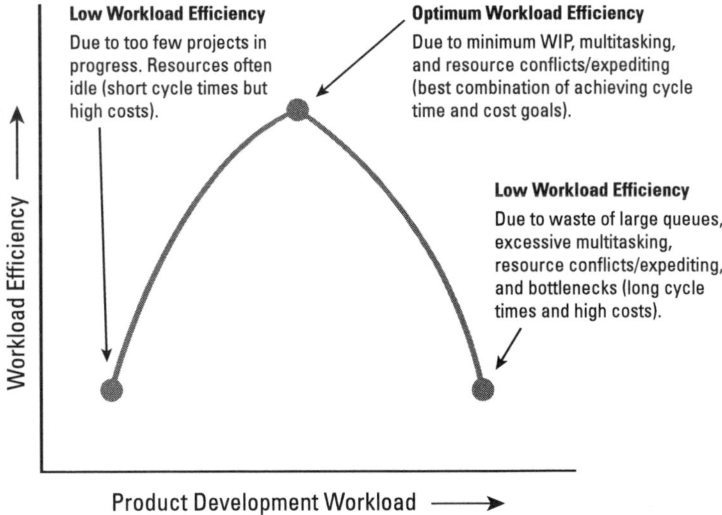

Figure 6-3. Improvement Strategy for Resource and Workload Management

IMPLEMENTING RESOURCE AND WORKLOAD MANAGEMENT

Implementing resource and workload management is depicted with the process shown in Figure 6-4. As you can see, implementation is facilitated through two elements designated as control points within the process: pipeline demand and capacity management, and work management.

Element #1: Pipeline Demand and Capacity Management

Pipeline demand and capacity management is an activity to prioritize and control the level of work going into a process. Incoming work is unpredictable. It fluctuates based on many factors, some of which the company can control and others that it cannot. Without a process to monitor the level of incoming work, the company would experience many of the problems already discussed related to multitasking, process bottlenecks, and so on.

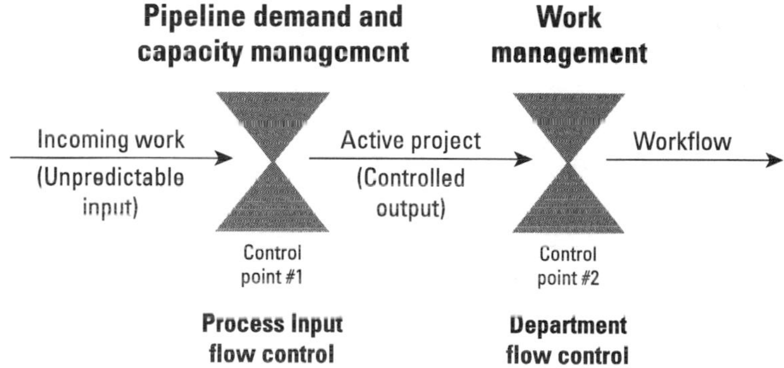

Figure 6-4. Implementing Resource and Workload Management

The primary goal of pipeline demand and capacity management is to ensure that work demand does not exceed available resource capacity. This element acts as a process input flow control by monitoring and releasing projects into the pipeline at times when the product development process can accommodate the work. Towards that end, projects are released only when available capacity exists. The highest value projects are identified and worked first, with the expectation that the execution of all released projects will be completed on time and within budget.

Typically, pipeline demand and capacity management is facilitated through a monthly meeting of product development and business management leaders. In one respect, the meeting essentially represents a partnership between the engineering and business functions within a company. The objective of this meeting is to review data related to upcoming projects and new business projections, resource staffing levels, and the current demand and capacity assessment. If you think about it, the practice of releasing work under the philosophy of pipeline demand and capacity management is analogous to the practice in manufacturing of not releasing an inventory of parts for the assembly-build of a product until all of the parts are available.

Element #2: Work Management

Work management is an activity to improve productivity and decrease cycle time by managing work at the department level. This element acts as a department flow control by managing work queues at the points where work comes into the department. In addition, work management strives to:

- Manage resources in the department to minimize multitasking and competition for resources
- Match department work demand to resource capacity
- Prioritize and integrate urgent, unplanned work into the department plan
- Identify and mitigate department bottlenecks and backlog issues
- Drive accountability in meeting the department work plan

There are two models for managing department workload. The need for different models is based on two factors: (1) the nature of the work tasks performed within the department and (2) the different entry points for receiving work.

Centralized Work Management

The first model is known as centralized work management and is depicted in Figure 6-5. This model is conducive to highly repetitive work tasks. In this model, the department manager, or focal point, is designated for receiving incoming work. This person is responsible for managing the work queue and distributing the work among the pool of available department resources. Based on this role, the manager has direct influence over issues related to multitasking and expediting. In theory, the manager should not assign a new job to a worker unless the prior job is completed.

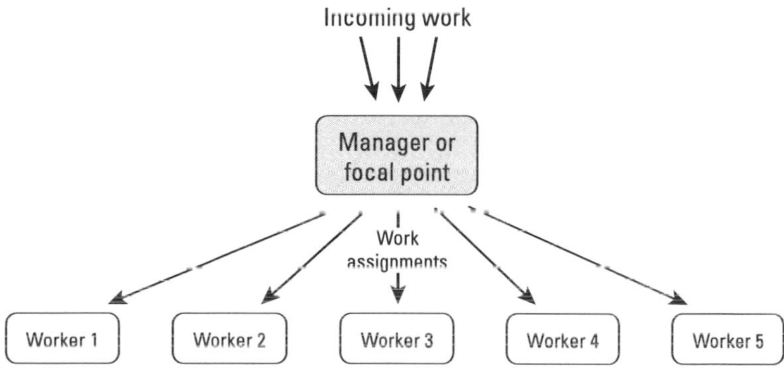

Figure 6-5. Centralized Work Management

This model is effective when the manager has the flexibility to assign a particular job to any worker from among a pool of capable resources. In this respect, the manager can use resources with the greatest latitude to satisfy the work demands of the department. Based on the flow of work illustrated in Figure 6-4, the model emulates a top-down approach to workload management.

Consolidated Work Management

The second model is known as consolidated work management and is shown in Figure 6-6. Compared to the centralized work management approach, consolidated work management is conducive to more specialized work tasks. In this case, department workload commitments must be segregated and completed by different workers with specific skill sets.

For example, consider a department responsible for performing engineering analysis of new product designs. Based on the requirement to perform a variety of different analysis, the department is staffed with stress analysts, reliability engineers, and materials engineers. To perform a stress analysis, for example, the stress analysts are obviously the only resources capable of completing the task. Based on the degree of specialization of workers with this model, the incoming work assignments for the department are often not received directly by a manager or work focal point, but rather by the individual workers who are members of project teams and who receive their work assignments directly from the teams.

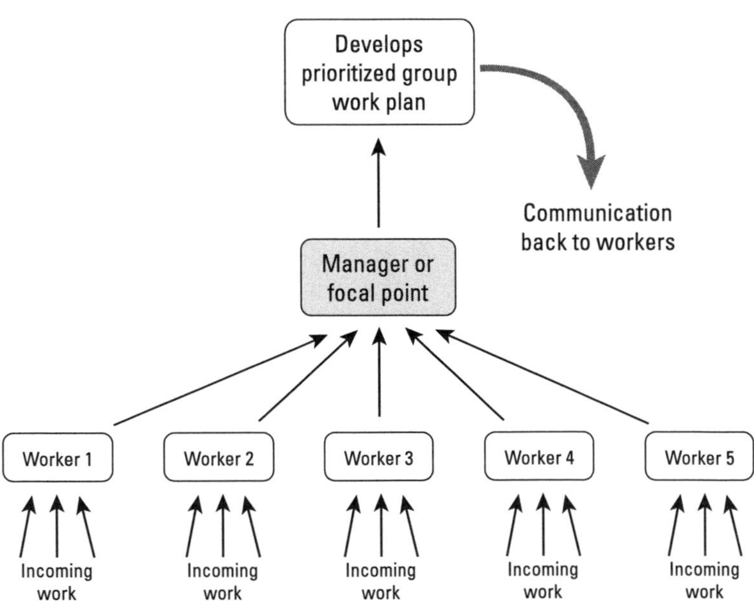

Figure 6-6. Consolidated Work Management

In this model, the individual workers communicate their work assignments to the manager or focal point. This communication is facilitated through the use of a simple spreadsheet filled out by the individual workers; this spreadsheet contains such information as the description of the work task, the project's required completion date, and the individual's estimated hours to complete. Once the information is collected, the manager evaluates the individual assignments and develops an overall department work plan. This plan is based on the manager's view of the organization's project priorities and the department's scheduling commitments. Once complete, the manager communicates the plan and work assignment priorities to the individuals in the department. Compared to the centralized model, the flow of work in this model emulates more of a bottoms-up approach to workload management.

Based on department dynamics and the continually changing environment associated with resource and workload management, the process outlined by the consolidated work management model is repeated on a weekly basis. Experience has shown the frequency of weekly updates to be extremely effective.

Resource and workload management is a fundamental element in terms of process improvement. Implementation of a work management model is relatively easy and fast, and improvement in efficiency and resource capacity can be realized almost immediately. Resource and workload management represents the starting point for process improvement, and in terms of the house of product development introduced in Chapter 5, is the first step in building the foundation shown in Figure 6-7.

Stability
(Foundation for improvement)

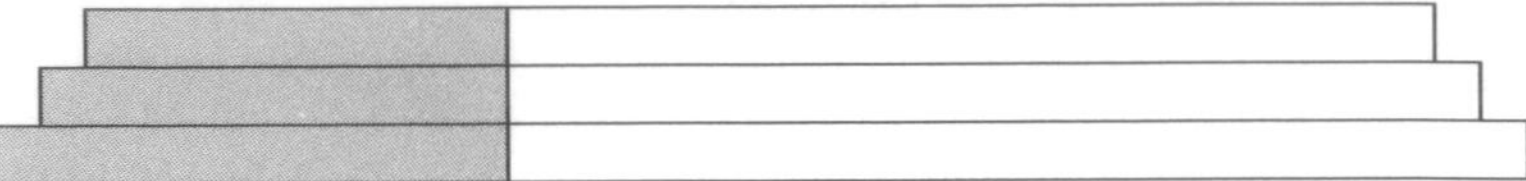

Resource & Workload Management
- Pipeline demand and capacity management
- Work management

Figure 6-7. Building the Foundation

Chapter 7 introduces another fundamental element required for improvement in the product development process: the concept of reuse.

CHAPTER 7

Implementing a Reuse Strategy

Unnecessary product variation is a major form of waste in product development. This waste comes from several issues related to managing large volumes of different parts, including:

- High product cost resulting from producing and procuring a variety of different parts in low volumes
- Parts management issues related to shortages, stocking, and requisitioning parts
- Numerous design quality issues
- High levels of production support, product upgrade issues, etc.

The solution to these problems is the implementation of a product reuse strategy. If you recall the ideas for product development outlined in Chapter 3, a product reuse strategy employs the guiding principle of reusing knowledge. A product reuse strategy is based on a simple premise:

> *The more a company can leverage its existing products, knowledge, and expertise in support of new product designs, the more it can circumvent the need to invest resources, time, and effort in creating those products, thereby reducing development cycle time and the associated costs.*

A reuse strategy also provides the benefit of reducing part cost through higher volume purchases of a subset of parts. In addition, it curtails the need for creating new parts, thereby reducing product variation within the company.

THE IMPACT OF A NEW PART ON THE COMPANY

A product development organization operates under the charter of creating new products and parts. Historically, this purpose has served companies very well. It's no secret that engineers and designers like to create new parts. When a new product or part is created, it is intended to serve a specific purpose that will ultimately provide value for the customer and translate into a profit for the company.

To realize a profit, the monetary return from selling the part to the customer must exceed the overall cost the company incurs by creating and maintaining the part itself. In light of today's cost-conscious business climate, companies need to be very sensitive to this issue. As a result, the engineers and designers who create products must be keenly sensitive to the cost implications of creating new parts.

As shown in Figure 7-1, a number of factors contribute to the cost of creating and maintaining a part. For some companies, the carrying cost alone for simply maintaining a part number in its system runs between $2000 and $3000 annually. Factoring in the non-recurring development cost as well as the manufacturing cost, the overall company expense of creating and maintaining parts is substantial. For these reasons, successful implementation of a product reuse strategy is a key enabler in reducing cost. To maximize the benefit from this strategy, employees involved in product development need to be educated about the financial implications for the company regarding maintaining parts, and become aware of the costs associated with creating new ones.

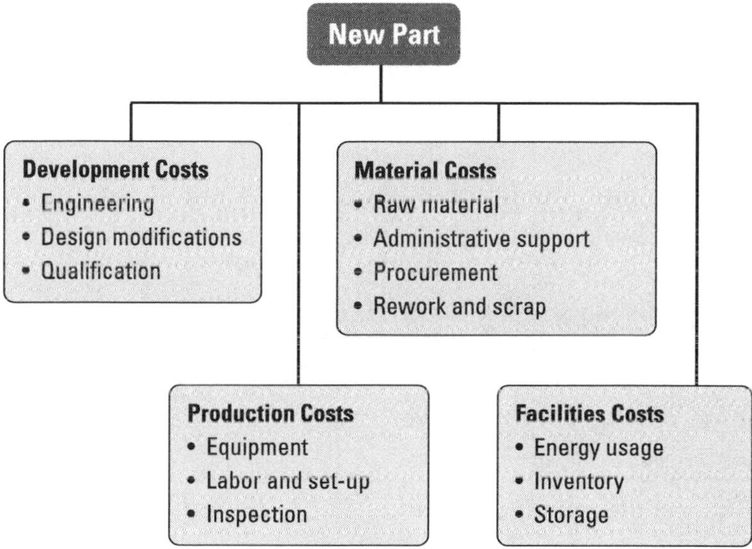

Figure 7-1. Impact of a New Part

Parts Reduction and Standardization

Parts reduction, coupled with elements of parts standardization, reduces variation for the parts a company manages. Activities that drive part-count reduction and standardization can provide additional benefits for the company, including:

- Reduced product complexity
- Improved product reliability
- Faster response to customer orders
- Faster time-to-market with new products
- Lower product development risk
- Easier product assembly

Parts reduction and standardization is an integral part of a product reuse strategy. This philosophy should not only extend to new products the company creates, but should also be considered for eliminating parts and reducing the overall parts count for products the company has already produced.

To determine if a part is a candidate for elimination, the following questions should be asked:

- Does the part move relative to the mating part?
- Must the part be a different material or be isolated from the mating part?
- Must the part be separate because of assembly requirements or does it need to be disassembled for service?
- Does the customer require it?

If the answer is "no" to all of these questions, the part is a prime candidate for consolidation or elimination.

There are various tools available to help evaluate opportunities for part reduction. These include tools ranging from simple spreadsheets that help assess parts to more sophisticated and commercially available tools that specialize in design for manufacture and assembly (DFMA).

IDENTIFYING PREFERRED PARTS

As stated previously, the goal of a product reuse strategy is to reduce product variation by consolidating the number of parts managed by a company. Therefore, a logical question to ask is how does a company determine which parts to use in support of a reuse strategy. The answer is by identifying and selecting preferred parts.

A *preferred part* is nothing more than a designation or label associated with an existing part design that has been identified with high reuse potential, that is, a part design with a high probability of use in a new product application. Preferred parts provide visibility to the product development organization for parts that represent the best characteristics in product performance and maximize value for the company. Consequently, in addition to traditional engineering considerations, the criteria for selecting preferred parts includes business considerations such as part cost, usage requirements, and manufacturing capability.

Preferred parts are typically identified as a subset of a larger part family. A *part family* is a grouping of parts with similar physical characteristics intended to perform the same basic function. For example, consider the collection of different bolts as shown in Figure 7-2. As you can see, this grouping contains bolts of different styles and sizes. These differences drive the use of specific bolts for particular applications. Collectively, however, this group of parts represents essentially one basic design performing the same basic function—to fasten other parts together. Consequently, the collection of bolts can be considered a part family.

Determining parts to be included in a family is somewhat subjective and depends on the nature of the parts being considered. However, identifying part families is the first step in assessing part variation within a company.

Figure 7-2. Part Family of Bolts

The Reuse Process

An effective product reuse strategy attempts to maximize utilization of the company's existing product portfolio through the identification of preferred parts. In order to facilitate this approach, the product development organization must have knowledge about the existing products and parts that it can leverage in support of the reuse strategy. The ability to acquire this knowledge is facilitated through part data that is collected through the reuse process. The *reuse process*, depicted in Figure 7-3, employs five key steps that culminate with the selection of preferred parts.

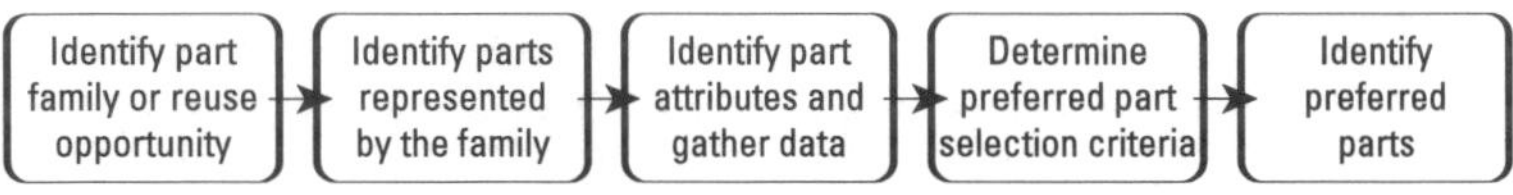

Figure 7-3. The Reuse Process

Step 1: Identify Part Family or Reuse Opportunity

This refers to a specific part family or any other high-value opportunity the company identifies to reduce product variation. Depending on the company's structure, the reuse opportunity may be associated with a particular product line or even a product area.

Step 2: Identify Parts Represented by the Family

Once the company has identified the opportunities for reducing product variation, the second step is to identify all of the individual parts represented by the family or reuse opportunity. There are a number of ways to accomplish this, but it really depends on how much information is already known about the parts that comprise the family. For example, some companies perform nomenclature searches within their enterprise resource planning (ERP) system, which enables the company to identify a particular type of part matching a specific description.

Step 3: Identify Part Attributes and Gather Data

The third step is to identify the part attributes and gather data for the identified parts. An *attribute* is simply a characteristic or piece of information that describes a product or part. From an engineering perspective, attributes include physical characteristics, dimensional data, performance parameters, operating conditions, material designations, configuration types, or any other pertinent part or product information. However, part attributes can also include information and characteristics about parts that extend beyond engineering such as part cost, historical parts usage, quality history, manufacturing capability, customer preferences, and so on. In summary, the selection of part attributes should include engineering, manufacturing, and other pertinent business-related information to enable a comprehensive assessment of a part's reuse potential.

The complexity of the part influences the amount of part attribute data that is collected. Typically, the more complex the part is, the more data that is needed to assess reuse potential. Regarding a reuse strategy, attribute data provides the means for quickly assessing existing parts for potential use in new product applications. Data elements such as cost data, usage data, quality data, etc., can often be obtained directly from other data sources or systems within the company (this will be explored in more detail in Chapter 10). However, for many companies, engineering part data is often not captured or readily available in support of a reuse philosophy.

Historically, for many companies involved in product development, the business model for the engineering department has been to finish one project, throw it over the wall to the manufacturing and procurement organizations, and then move on to the next project. Consequently, operating under this approach, product development organizations have not developed feedback mechanisms that provide information regarding the effectiveness of completed product designs or an infrastructure that captures part data. Based on this, the need to capture and use engineering part attribute data to support reuse is critically important for many companies in order to fill the void generated from deficient feedback mechanisms.

A company should use discretion regarding the quantity of attributes that are selected for a specific part family. The goal is to capture enough attributes so there is adequate detail in the part data in order to select a few key candidate parts with reuse potential. However, selecting too many attributes for a part family introduces two issues. First, the amount of part data that is generated from many attributes could overwhelm a user in terms of the amount of information that would need to be analyzed for a reuse opportunity. Second, a large number of attributes increases the initial task of collecting and gathering the part data for the family. However, selecting too few attributes for a family could result in a collection of part data that would be too vague for a practitioner to identify parts with reuse potential.

Once the attributes are determined, the specific data for the parts represented by the family can be captured and cataloged. Typically, most part data is derived from engineering drawings for the part or product, but it may also come from other sources. Ultimately, the specific sources for capturing the part data depends on the attribute.

The use of simple spreadsheets can facilitate the initial task of capturing and cataloging part data based on attributes. Figure 7-4 provides an example of a spreadsheet format that has worked very effectively for many companies. The attributes for the part family are represented as the column headings, with

Part Number	Attribute 1	Attribute 2	Attribute 3	Attribute 4	Attribute 5
Part 1					
Part 2					
Part 3					
Part 4					
Part 5					
Part 6					
Part 7					
Part 8					

Figure 7-4. Spreadsheet Format for Cataloging Part Data

the part numbers listed in the left-hand column. The body of the spreadsheet would contain the attribute data captured for each specific part. The number of attributes and individual part numbers represented by the specific family dictate the overall size of the spreadsheet.

This step of the reuse process, dealing with attribute identification and data collection, embodies the concept of group technology. *Group technology* is a management philosophy based on leveraging similarities in the design and manufacture of parts for the purpose of performing a known function. In terms of the reuse process, this step generates attribute data as the basis for understanding part similarities and is a precursor for selecting preferred parts.

Step 4: Determine Preferred Part Selection Criteria

The specific criterion is unique to each part family and depends on the characteristics and functional requirements of the parts However, the following general guidelines can be used when selecting preferred parts:

- Select high-usage, low-cost parts
- Select commercially available parts when possible (i.e., avoid obsolete and specialty parts)
- Consider the manufacturing implications and downstream users of the parts
- Consider customer preferences and industry trends
- Select parts based on engineering best practices

Step 5: Identify Preferred Parts

Typically, product development practitioners with intimate knowledge about the parts and the part family are chartered with making the selections. In addition, depending on the part family, it may be prudent to consult with downstream users of the preferred parts such as mechanics or service technicians to gain their perspective and validate the selections.

Applying the Reuse Process to Software Development

Elements of the reuse process can be easily adapted to support the needs of software development. For example, a block of code used in a program (software) is analogous to an individual part used to create a product (hardware). As a result, blocks of code with reuse potential can be characterized based on attributes that describe their functional intent. Like parts, certain blocks of code with high reuse potential can be captured, cataloged, and designated as preferred.

The same issues regarding deficient feedback mechanisms also plague software development. In response, an effective way for software developers to gain insight and feedback regarding newly developed code is to monitor the software support desk for a period of time after the code's release. By doing this, developers can obtain first-hand information from the customers and users regarding the effectiveness and success of their products.

Creating a Preferred Part Index

As a company undertakes the task of implementing a reuse strategy, it becomes necessary for it to manage the pool of preferred parts that have been selected. Over time, it may be necessary to add or delete preferred parts due to a variety of reasons such as part availability or changes in market trends.

For many companies, a mechanism used to help manage preferred parts is a preferred part index (PPI). A preferred part index is a document containing the listing of all preferred parts identified by the company. The document is typically placed under the company's document management system and treated like any other document or specification under revision control. By doing so, the company can manage and maintain the current version of the preferred parts index as changes are made over time.

THE PRODUCT PORTFOLIO

In order for a company to address the issue of product variation, it is important for the company to understand the composition of products and parts that make up its *product portfolio*. For a typical company, commodity parts and consumables represent the largest category of parts (by volume) maintained by the company. This category of parts represents items such as nuts, bolts, screws, diodes, capacitors, lubricants, greases, compounds, paints, and so on.

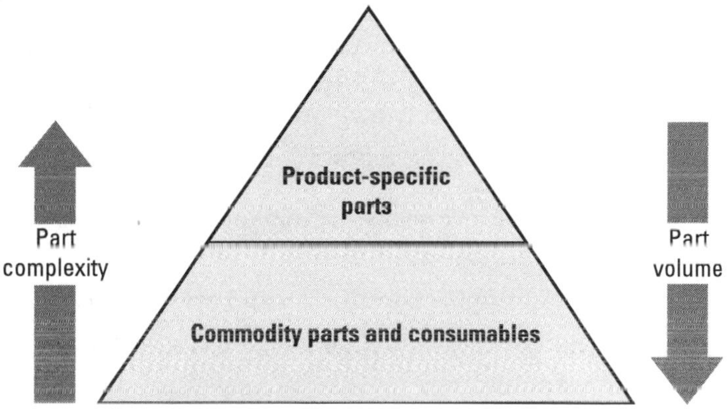

Figure 7-5. Typical Company Parts Portfolio

A smaller category of parts represents the product-specific parts that are designed by the company. This concept can be summed up in terms of the illustration in Figure 7-5. As you can see, the arrows indicate an inverse relationship between the part complexity and the total volume of parts supported by a company. The triangular shape representing the parts portfolio is intended to further illustrate this relationship.

Commodity Parts and Consumables

Except for companies that specifically produce these components, *commodity parts and consumables* are typically off-the-shelf items purchased by companies to support products they produce. For example, consider a company that designs and manufactures bicycles. The company will design the product-specific parts of the bicycle, such as the frame, wheels, brake assembly, and so on. But the commodity-type parts such as nuts, bolts, screws, and so on that are needed to assemble the bicycle, will most likely not be designed by the bicycle company, but rather purchased from companies that specialize in the manufacture of these components.

Implementation of a product reuse strategy initially focused on commodity parts and consumables is the first step in eliminating unnecessary product variation. In addition, this activity addresses a number of fundamental issues necessary for improvement in the product development process. This initial implementation provides the following benefits:

- Introduces the basic process elements in the selection and reuse of preferred parts
- Promotes linkage in the value chain between the product development and procurement organizations for parts procurement and use
- Initiates a cultural change within the product development organization from creation to reuse

Increasing the Use of Commodity Parts and Consumables

Commodity parts and consumables are by their very nature, simple parts. These parts represent basic designs that are easily interchangeable. This simplicity provides a unique opportunity for a company to use preferred parts of this type, not only for new designs, but also for existing products produced by the company. Consequently, consideration should be given to the opportunity for using preferred commodity parts and consumables in designs of products currently being manufactured by the company. By taking advantage of this opportunity, the company could dramatically increase the usage of preferred parts in a relatively short period of time. This utilization increase would translate into higher volume purchases, which would further reduce part cost.

Product-Specific Parts

Product-specific parts represent a higher level of part complexity, but typically reflect the smaller category in a company's product portfolio. Consequently, this category of parts represents the second phase of implementation regarding a product reuse strategy. As a result of using the reuse process and identifying preferred parts for each category within the company's product portfolio, subcategories within the company's parts portfolio are created as shown in Figure 7-6.

Notice that the product-specific parts category has been split into two categories known as strategic parts and core parts. Strategic parts represent a small subset of the company's core or product-specific parts, which possess unique technical requirements or provide the company with a unique competitive advantage for the products it produces.

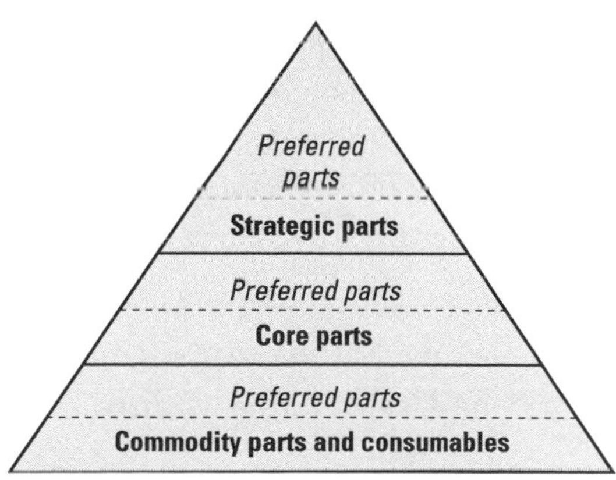

Figure 7-6. Modified Company Parts Portfolio

In terms of a reuse strategy, selecting preferred parts creates a hierarchy of reuse. For example, consider the creation of a new product requiring a shaft component. Using a hierarchical approach, the first choice would be to select a preferred part for use in the new product design. However, if no preferred shafts were acceptable, the second choice would be to select an existing non-preferred shaft.[1] From the company's perspective, this is still better than creating a new part. Lastly, if no existing non-preferred parts were acceptable, then the only recourse would be to design a new part.

ACTIVITY-BASED COSTING

The danger in promoting high-cost parts through a reuse strategy can undermine the economic benefits from its implementation. Consequently, companies must have a fundamental understanding of the true cost of their parts to implement a successful reuse program.

Many companies employ accounting systems that make it difficult to assess actual part cost. In these systems, company overhead costs are blanketed across many parts, which masks the actual part cost. To overcome the deficiencies caused by these systems, companies can use activity-based costing.

Activity-based costing is an accounting method that allows a company to determine the actual cost associated with each product or service produced independent of the company's overhead cost structure. Activity-based costing can be summarized based on the following steps:

- Activities that consume resources are identified and costs are assigned to those activities.
- Cost drivers associated with each activity are identified.

---

1. Consideration must be given to avoid selecting non-preferred parts that cause product failures, possess high scrap rates, or any other product development or business consideration that would undermine the goals of a reuse strategy. Parts of this nature should be identified and noted during the data review for selecting preferred parts.

- A cost rate per cost driver (or transaction) is computed.
- Costs are assigned to a product by multiplying the cost driver rate by the volume of cost driver units consumed by the product.

Activity-based costing represents a viable approach to determine what parts really cost. Companies employing a reuse strategy should consider this accounting method to support their implementation plan.

To summarize, implementation of a product reuse strategy provides the benefit of initiating the transformation within the product development organization from a design philosophy of creation to one of reuse. The two-phased implementation, addressing commodity parts and consumables and product-specific parts, enables the company to assess its product portfolio and address product variation. The task of collecting and cataloging part data through the reuse process can be, at times, a somewhat arduous task. However, experience has clearly shown that gathering and capturing part data is an investment that pays enormous dividends. Part data represents a valuable resource that supports follow-up activities that translate into significant reductions in product development cycle time and cost.

A product reuse strategy is a fundamental element that enables implementation of subsequent activities such as with design process selection, integration of manufacturing and the company's supply chain, and implementation of Manufacturing Process Control and Design for Six Sigma. These topics will be addressed in Chapters 9, 11, 12, and 13.

In conclusion, reuse concepts represent the starting point for reducing product variation. In addition, these concepts set in motion the process and cultural changes in the organization that are required for real improvement. Regarding the house of product development introduced in Chapter 5, reuse concepts continue to build on the foundational elements necessary for improvement in product development, as shown in Figure 7-7.

Stability

(Foundation for improvement)

Resource & Workload Management
- Pipeline demand and capacity management
- Work management

Reuse Concepts
- Part family identification
- Preferred parts selection
- Product portfolio assessment

Figure 7-7. Continuing to Build the Foundation

Chapter 8 introduces the last fundamental element needed for improvement in the product development process: building the correct level of process infrastructure, which will ensure that improvements are properly monitored and sustained.

CHAPTER 8

Building the Infrastructure for Product Development

The ability to effectively manage a project is key to its success. Effective management strives to ensure the project is properly staffed with required and capable resources, has an adequate budget based on the project scope, and is supported by a plan with established milestones and targeted completion dates. These elements represent the fundamentals of program management.

As a project is executed, effective program management requires periodic reviews to ensure that progress on the project agrees with the established plan. Consequently, it is necessary for a company to have adequate checks and balances in its processes to monitor the progress of projects against these plans. This is indeed the case with product development. These checks and balances represent a level of process infrastructure that must be developed and integrated with the product development process.

The goal for a company is to achieve the correct level of process infrastructure. Too little infrastructure does not promote adequate discipline in company processes for completing projects, thereby resulting in unnecessary variation and excessive amounts of waste. Too much infrastructure is in itself wasteful, because it requires excessive amounts of non-value-added work in preparing and participating in the review process. The trap in following this approach is the tendency to inspect in quality. Consequently, business requirements and the maturity of the process determine the appropriate level of process infrastructure and the specific elements that are needed. For instance, the need for process discipline is typically high in the early stages of a company's introduction of lean concepts, and this need reduces as the process matures and a new culture evolves.

THE INFRASTRUCTURE FOR PRODUCT DEVELOPMENT

As shown in Figure 8-1, successful product development requires infrastructure support from three core areas: project management, design assurance, and resource and workload management. Chapter 6 was devoted entirely to outlining the objectives and process for implementing resource and workload management, so there is no need to elaborate further on that subject in this chapter. However, it is important to recognize that resource and workload management play an integral part in terms of the overall process infrastructure for product development. Also, note in Figure 8-1 the relationship of the core elements and the supporting processes within product development. This linkage helps to maintain the discipline needed to ensure successful project completion.

The balance of this chapter focuses on addressing the other core elements of the process infrastructure: project management and design assurance.

PROJECT MANAGEMENT

The objective of the project management infrastructure is to insure that projects meet their overall objectives in terms of scope, cost, and schedule. Project management is composed of three elements:

1. Project management process
2. Project reviews
3. Management reviews

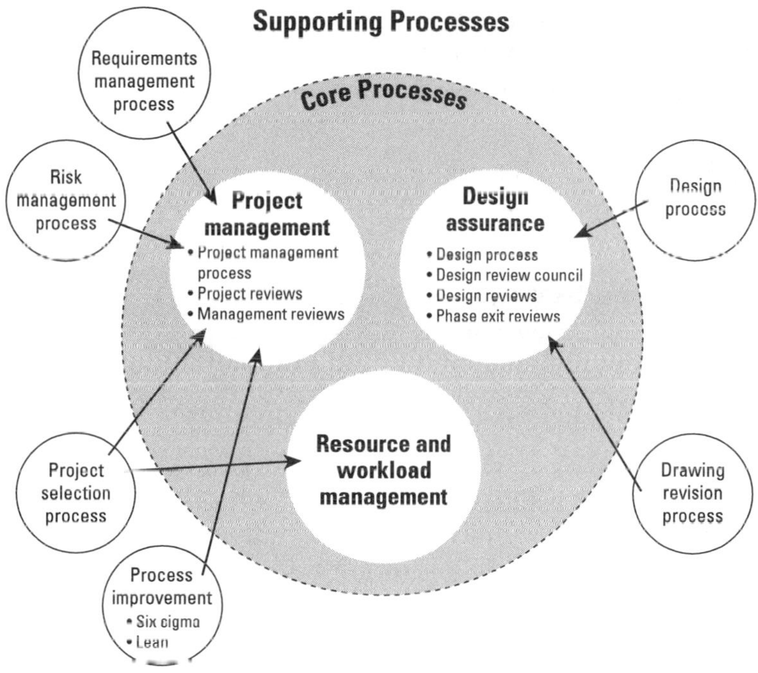

Figure 8-1. Product Development Process Infrastructure

Let's take a look at the requirements of each element:

The Project Management Process

This element deals with identifying and documenting the project management process that a company uses. This includes the structure and frequency for conducting reviews as well as identifying the tools, templates, and metrics to be measured and reported. Additionally, this element includes support for maintaining the process and training of employees in using the process.

Project Reviews

This element deals with conducting structured and periodic reviews in accordance with the project management process. The objective of these reviews is to assess a project's progress in meeting established goals. The reviews typically follow a standardized reporting format, with supporting metrics that measure a project's progress in meeting an established plan. Consequently, a key outcome of project reviews is to identify areas that do not conform to the schedule and then to develop a gap-closure strategy.

Management Reviews

These are higher-level management reviews intended to assess the overall health of the projects currently being worked. The goal of a management review is to identify projects that are at risk and to develop risk-mitigation plans.

As mentioned earlier, metrics play a key role in the project management review process in terms of assessing the current state of a project. Here is a listing of typical metrics that may be included in a project review:

- Schedule adherence to a project plan (cycle time)
- Budget adherence to a project plan
- Design-to-cost adherence
- Project risk rating
- Technical requirements assessment (unresolved requirements, etc.)

DESIGN ASSURANCE

The objective of the design assurance infrastructure is to ensure adherence to the product development design process. Elements under design assurance include:

- The design process selection
- The design review council
- Design reviews
- Phase exit reviews

Let's look at each element in more detail.

The Design Process Selection

This element deals with the selecting the appropriate design strategy for a particular project. Products can be designed using a modular, platform, or custom design approach. Two factors that influence the design approach are the product's assembly characteristics and the company's experience regarding the particular product. (These topics will be discussed in greater detail in Chapter 9.) In addition, this element involves identifying the design tools needed to support the process, along with training and mentoring the product development organization regarding the design process.

The Design Review Council

The charter for the design review council is to establish, identify, and maintain engineering best practices in support of new product design. An engineering best practice can represent a product or part, as in the case of preferred parts, or a methodology in support of product development. The council is chaired by the product development organization's primary technology leader, and the staff are other technical lead engineers.

Design Reviews

This element deals with conducting a formal meeting, or review, intended to ensure that the product design conforms to the technical requirements dictated by the customer. Depending on the nature of the business and the type of product being developed, multiple design reviews may be conducted throughout the product development process. For example, in the aircraft industry, it is not uncommon for companies to conduct a preliminary design review early in the process, after the conceptual design phase. Then, to conduct a subsequent critical design review later on in the process, after the creation of the detail drawings. In addition, in some cases, the customers themselves may participate in the design review meetings.

The design review meeting is structured around a checklist-driven format. In other words, the product development team arrives at the design review with a completed checklist for a particular project. The checklist represents standard activities and tasks that need to be completed as part of the overall design process and represents the basis for discussion during the design review meeting. The team presents to management the objective evidence of completed items documented on the checklist, and any open items or design issues that need to be addressed.

Phase Exit Reviews

Phase exit reviews are intended to ensure that the product design adheres to the phase exit criteria established by the design process. Typically, the phase exit criteria is structured and also checklist-driven. Many times, to streamline the overall project management process, the phase exit reviews are combined with the project reviews.

In summary, developing a process infrastructure is a key enabler for process improvement. Achieving the correct level in product development helps instill the appropriate measure of discipline in the process. Related to the house of product development that was introduced in Chapter 5, developing a process infrastructure completes the foundational elements needed for improvement, as shown in Figure 8-2.

Stability
(Foundation for improvement)

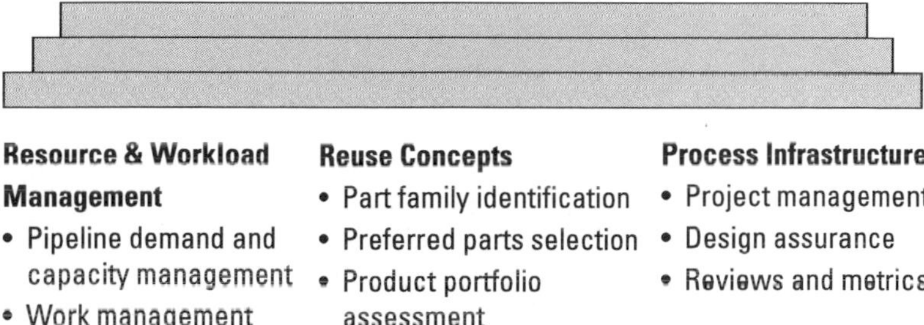

Figure 8-2. Completing the Foundation

This chapter concludes the section for stabilizing the product development process. Part Four streamlines the product development process, beginning with "Chapter 9: Selecting the Appropriate Design Strategy."

PART FOUR

Streamlining the Product Development Process

Part Four describes three areas that facilitate additional improvement in the product development process: selecting the appropriate design strategy, developing software tools, and integrating the supply chain.

CHAPTER 9

Selecting the Appropriate Design Strategy

Chapter 7 expounded on the issues resulting from excessive product variation. However, in addition to product variation, another key contributor to high product cost and poor design quality is excessive process variation. Unnecessary process variation promotes waste in the product development process. Examples of this include:

- Designing a new part when an equivalent one already exists
- Using multiple methods for performing standard engineering analysis
- Recreating product data

However, it is important to note that these statements do not advocate a one-size-fits-all approach to product development. By their very nature, products possess different characteristics, which influence how individual parts within a product function and relate to one another, how the product is assembled, and, ultimately, how the product is designed. As a result, companies need to be flexible and select a design approach that most closely aligns with the characteristics of the product, so that the company can maximize profitability and customer value. Companies that have integrated their design process with the lean fundamentals and guiding principles (presented in Chapters 2 and 3) have achieved dramatic results. These results include:

- 70 percent reduction in product development cycle time
- 50 percent reduction in product cost
- 5 sigma design quality level
- 90 percent conformance of design-to-cost targets

THREE DESIGN STRATEGIES

As stated earlier, products possess different characteristics that influence the design approach. These characteristics are summarized in terms of three design strategies: modular, platform, or custom. Evaluating these against the backdrop of development cycle time and the concept of reuse, the design strategies can be compared, as shown in Figure 9-1.

This graphic shows that development cycle time increases along the horizontal axis from left to right. This also equates to product cost and technical risk. Along the vertical axis is reuse, which relates to part designs as well as discipline in following the product development process. This level increases from the bottom to the top. Within the body of the chart, the three strategies for product design are referenced. Notice that with regard to the horizontal and vertical axes, the strategies cover the spectrum of development cycle time and reuse.

Many companies that lack discipline in their product development process operate almost exclusively in the lower right region of the chart, where part reuse and process conformance is low, and consequently, product cost and cycle times are high. However, employing lean principles and the reuse process (discussed in Chapter 7) has provided companies the flexibility to operate in the middle and upper left regions of the chart, where reuse and process discipline is higher, and cycle time and product cost is lower.

Companies may not operate exclusively utilizing a modular, platform, or custom design strategy. As mentioned at the beginning of this chapter, this decision is influenced not only by product characteristics, but also by the company's technical

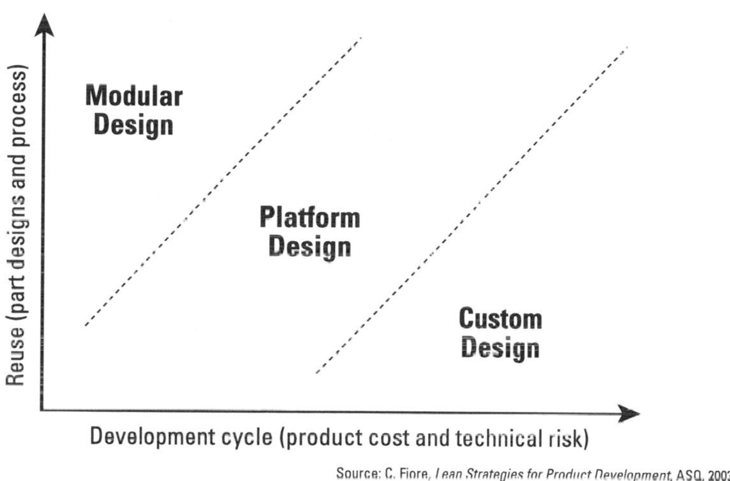

Figure 9-1. Comparison of the Three Product Design Strategies

expertise, product knowledge, and its relative position in the marketplace. As a result, the transition between the three strategies is somewhat fuzzy. This is graphically represented in Figure 9-1 by the dashed lines separating the approaches. To further clarify these statements, let's take a look at each of the three design strategies in more detail.

OPTION #1: MODULAR DESIGN

The term *modular design* is derived from the word "module" or "subassembly." In other words, the modular approach is essentially a design strategy based on using *modules*, or subassemblies. To illustrate this approach, consider an automobile. An automobile can be divided into various subassemblies, such as the engine, frame assembly, steering column assembly, passenger seat assembly, dashboard assembly, and so on. There are many other examples of products that exhibit modular characteristics, such as personal computers, kitchen appliances, power tools, bicycles, and even the International Space Station, which was transported and assembled in space using a modular approach.

Products conducive to modular design exhibit certain characteristics. Typically, products of this type can have their overall performance altered through the use of modules with different performance characteristics. As a result, modules can be changed using a plug-and-play approach. For example, consider a personal computer. To improve computer response time, the processor module can be replaced with one possessing a higher central processing unit (CPU) rating. All other parts of the computer can still be used. However, to achieve extensive use of modules, a key enabler is to standardize the interfaces between modules and their mating parts to ensure a high degree of interchangeability.

In practical application of the modular design approach, it is probably unrealistic to create new products exclusively from modules. In reality, a combination of modules, preferred parts, non-preferred parts, and newly designed parts is more feasible. However, the goal in using the modular design approach is to achieve the highest level of module and preferred parts usage, in order to maximize the benefits of reduced cycle time and cost. Consequently, this approach makes extensive use of the reuse process outlined in Chapter 7.

The modular design process is depicted in Figure 9-2, which clearly exemplifies the hierarchy of reuse discussed earlier. Chapter 7 outlined the approach for identifying preferred parts. But a logical question to ask is: How do we identify module opportunities that support the creation of products using the modular design approach? The answer is through use of a tool known as a *product breakdown structure*.

A product breakdown structure is essentially a tree diagram that starts at the finished product level and breaks down the product into pieces that represent different levels. The module level represents subassemblies that can be created to support reuse opportunities in the modular design approach. To illustrate this concept, consider an automobile. Using a product

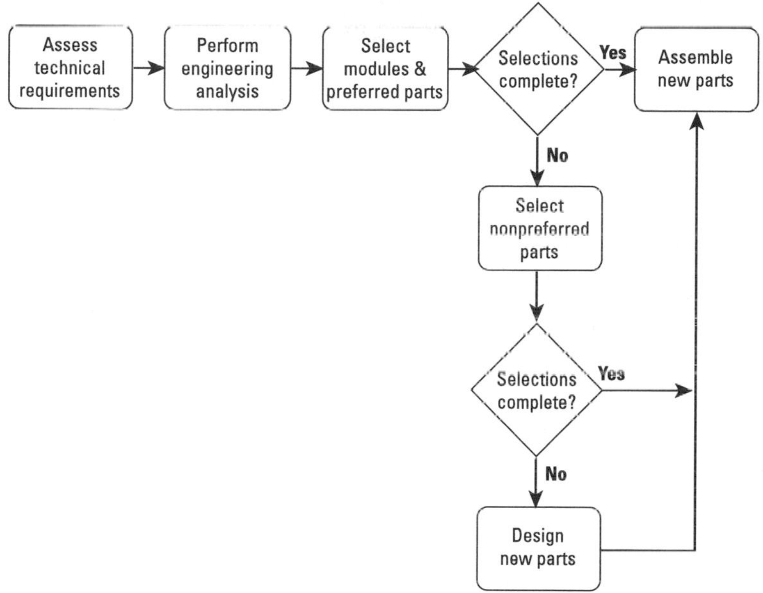

Figure 9-2. Modular Design Process

breakdown structure, an automobile may be decomposed into the form shown in Figure 9-3.

This is by no means a complete product breakdown structure for an automobile, but it does convey the concept of how one works. Starting at the product level, an automobile is divided into three pieces at the major assembly level. (In practice, each major assembly would be further subdivided, but this example focuses on only one level.) Next, the body is broken down into smaller pieces, represented by the module level. Finally, if necessary, the modules themselves can be broken down further into the various individual parts. The product breakdown structure is essentially a road map to identify reuse opportunities for a product. Logically, the more complex the product, the more complex the product breakdown structure will be.

The assembly of the product is a key factor and requires careful consideration when using a product breakdown structure to define modules. By ensuring that modules can be assembled,

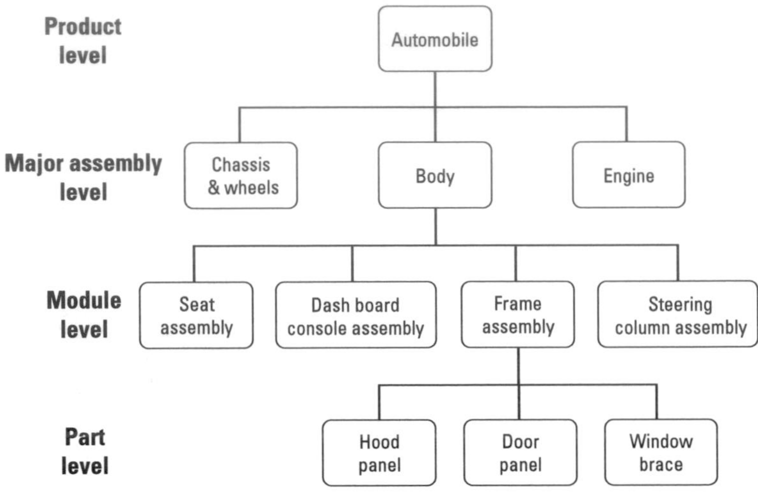

Figure 9-3. Example of a Product Breakdown Structure

a company can maximize the cost benefits by exploiting opportunities for procuring fully assembled modules from its supply base, instead of procuring or manufacturing individual parts. In this respect, the product breakdown structure helps to close the gap between how the product is assembled and how it should be designed. Armed with this information, the product development organization can use the product breakdown structure as the framework for creating the blueprint drawing package that defines the product.

Employing a modular design approach also has a significant impact on the company's product portfolio. As a result of creating modules, a new class in the portfolio is created. This is illustrated with an additional modification to the company parts portfolio shown in Figure 9-4.

As you can see in the graphic, by pooling parts from the strategic and core parts categories, a new module class is created. In terms of a hierarchy of reuse, modules, along with preferred parts that are identified for each category, represent the first option in utilizing parts under a reuse strategy.

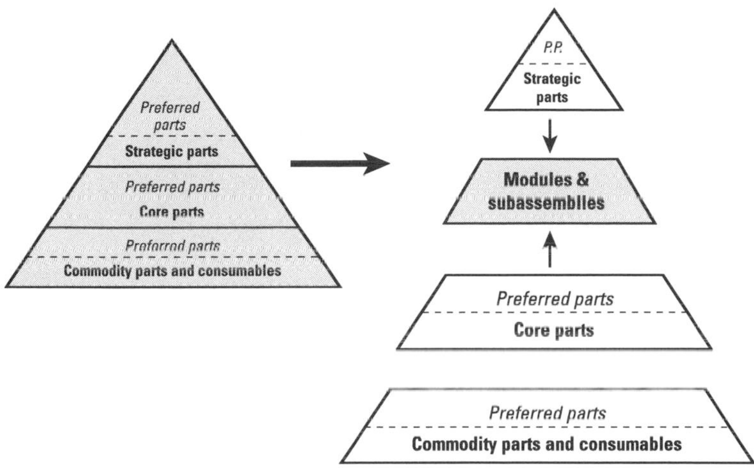

Figure 9-4. A Further Modified Company Parts Portfolio

OPTION #2: PLATFORM DESIGN

As just described, the modular design approach is based on the creation of modules or subassemblies; i.e., the logical grouping of parts that perform specific functions and that can be easily interchanged to alter overall product performance. Let's contrast this approach with that of a product supported by the *platform design* strategy. With this type of product, there is a higher degree of dependency between the individual components. All of the parts must work together to perform the product's primary function. Consequently, products of this nature are not conducive to the plug-and-play approach with modules.

A good example of a product fitting this strategy would be a commercial jet engine. In this case, the jet engine is designed to meet a certain thrust requirement. The individual parts all work in tandem and are sized to meet the requirement. Generally, it's not possible to replace or resize one or two parts to change the product's overall performance. It's kind of like a domino effect. If one part changes, it affects another, then another, and so on. In other words, the entire product represents a platform, or baseline design. If a different thrust requirement is needed, typically an entirely new product is created. In other words, the entire engine design needs to be scaled up or down to meet the different requirement.

The goals are the same for the platform design strategy in terms of reducing product development cycle time and cost, but the approach is indeed different. This approach is illustrated in Figure 9-5.

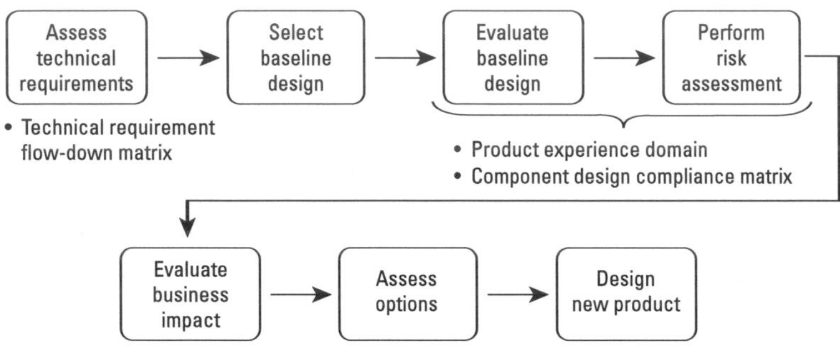

Figure 9-5. Platform Design Process

As opposed to reusing existing modules and parts, this approach results in creating a new product, one based on an existing design that represents the baseline, or starting point. Based on this, the platform approach also attempts to leverage the company's existing product portfolio in support of new design, but in a different way. The primary focus of the platform design strategy is to do the following:

- Follow a disciplined approach in managing and understanding technical risk
- Characterize a product's performance and known design space

Because a new product is being created, it is critically important that the new product perform as intended upon its inception, to avoid subsequent redesign. This is important not only from a customer satisfaction perspective, but also from a business perspective.

The platform design approach uses three tools to help manage the technical risk and characterize product performance:

- A technical requirements flow-down matrix
- A product experience domain
- A component design compliance matrix

The following sections take a closer look at each of these tools

Technical Requirements Flow-Down Matrix

The *technical requirements flow-down matrix* provides a consistent way to evaluate the technical requirements for a new product. The matrix performs three valuable functions:

- It helps instill discipline in the evaluation process.
- It standardizes the approach.
- When referenced against a baseline product, it promotes a clear understanding of the areas of non-compliance.

The matrix is structured using a simple spreadsheet format: see Figure 9-6.

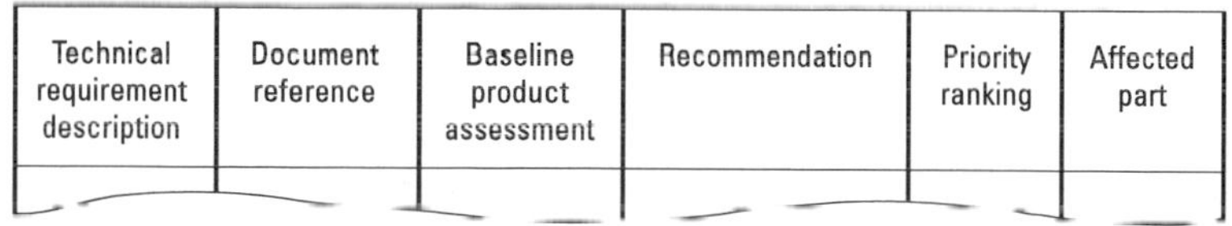

Technical requirement description	Document reference	Baseline product assessment	Recommendation	Priority ranking	Affected part

Source: C. Fiore, *Lean Strategies for Product Development*, ASQ, 2003

Figure 9-6. Technical Requirements Flow-Down Matrix

Each technical requirement is denoted on the matrix and measured against the characteristics of the selected baseline product design. In addition, after assessing the requirements against the baseline, the product development organization makes recommendations on how the requirements may be satisfied. This is based on priority ranking of the requirement and the criticality of the part affected by the requirement. The matrix also acts as a planning tool for identifying future activity. With a completed matrix, a company can identify gaps in meeting the technical requirements and then develop a plan to eliminate those gaps.

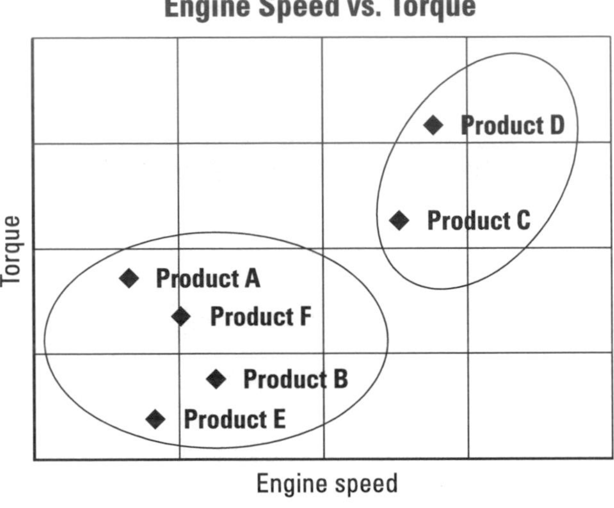

Figure 9-7. Product Experience Domain Example

Product Experience Domain

The *product experience domain* is a data set that can take on a couple of different forms:

- Cataloged data similar to that used for the modular design approach
- A data table
- Some type of graphical representation

Regardless of the form, the product experience domain represents information that characterizes key performance parameters of the company's existing products. In addition, product experience domains act as tools by helping the product development organization identify areas of risk for new product designs.

An example of a product experience domain is shown in Figure 9-7. Suppose we're evaluating performance parameters such as engine speed versus vibration. The graph shows the performance of six actual products for these parameters represented by products A through F. Using the scatter of the existing products on the graph, two distinct groups, represented by the circles, are formed. These circles represent the region or area of experience based on the performance of the existing products.

So now suppose a company is creating a new product. The performance of the new product for the parameters of engine speed and vibration would be derived and referenced against this product experience domain. If the data point for the new product falls within one of the circled regions, then the new product's performance is within the range of the company's experience and existing product portfolio in terms of this design parameter. There would be a high degree of certainty in terms of the product design and its performance with regard to this parameter.

However, if the data point falls outside of the circled regions, then the new product's performance is beyond the company's current experience level. This would imply that the new design poses some risk with regard to these performance parameters. The farther away the new product's data point is from the circled regions, the higher the degree of risk. At this point, the company would need to perform additional work to modify the product design and mitigate the risk or to assess the potential impact of the risk from a business and engineering perspective.

Successful characterizations of a company's products require the creation of a library of product experience domains for the key performance parameters. The time and effort spent creating product experience domains represents an investment by a company. This investment pays dividends, though, because product development practitioners who use product experience domains can better understand the capabilities of the products produced by their company. The more product development practitioners know about product capability, the better job they will do in the future in creating new products and having them work correctly the first time.

Component Design Compliance Matrix

Like the technical requirements of flow-down matrix, the *component design compliance matrix* is a tool arranged in a spreadsheet format. Its primary function is to help develop actions when component designs do not meet the minimum requirements. The key elements of a component design compliance matrix are shown in Figure 9-8.

Design requirement	Design criteria	Validation methodology	Rating to accepted standard	Experience	Proposed mitigation of noncompliance

Source: C. Fiore, *Lean Strategies for Product Development*, ASQ, 2003

Figure 9-8. A Component Design Compliance Matrix

The component design compliance matrix is another example of using a tool to instill a measure of consistency in the product development process. The design requirements for a specific component are listed in the matrix. In addition, information is documented to assess a company's ability to meet and verify the requirement. Finally, mitigation plans are noted to address areas of non-compliance. In terms of a new product design, a component design compliance matrix would be created for each new core or strategic part that needs to be created.

The tools used in the platform design approach facilitate a methodical and disciplined approach to creating a new product based on an existing design. To summarize and recap the tools:

- The technical requirements flow-down matrix instills consistency in evaluating customer needs and requirements for new products.

- The product experience domain characterizes the performance and experience base of existing products and helps identify areas of risk for new product designs.
- The component design compliance matrix provides a methodology to ensure that new component designs meet the minimum design requirements.

OPTION #3: CUSTOM DESIGN

Referring back to Figure 9-1, the custom design approach represents the lowest level of reuse and the highest level of product development cycle time and cost. On the surface, it appears this statement implies that companies should avoid using the custom design approach due to its tendency to promote product variation. However, this is not the case. A *custom design* strategy is a viable option when the variation adds value for the company. In other words, if a customer is willing to pay more for a special or customized product, then variation is justified.

For instance, consider the Wheels-R-Us Bicycle Company, which specializes in the design and manufacture of street-touring bicycles. For Wheels-R-Us, producing street-touring bicycles represents the company's core competency. In other words, Wheels-R-Us possesses a high level of skill, knowledge, and expertise, thereby enabling it to fulfill its mission of designing and manufacturing street touring bicycles.

In terms of a design strategy, Wheels-R-Us employs a modular design approach with heavy emphasis on a reuse process for creating new street-touring bicycles. Recently, Wheels-R-Us decided it wanted to expand its product portfolio beyond street-touring bicycles to include mountain bikes. However, a design strategy that leverages the company's existing product portfolio and employs a high level of part reuse would not be very useful for Wheels-R-Us in this application. Mountain bicycle frames are much sturdier than street-touring bicycle frames to endure the rugged terrain. In addition, mountain bicycles require more complex gearing systems, thicker tires, and a different handle bar design as compared to street bicycles. For these reasons, it's obvious that a mountain bike design represents a departure from Wheels-R-Us's core competencies associated with street-touring designs. The mountain bike requires Wheels-R-Us to design the product outside its existing core competency and beyond its present knowledge base and operating environment. This situation exemplifies a product requiring a custom design approach.

The custom design approach should be used to focus on the development of breakthrough products for a company. Breakthrough products represent innovative new products that add to a company's existing portfolio, or upgrades that enhance the capability of existing products to meet new customer demands or market needs. A custom design requires a company to extend beyond its known core competencies and, as a result, represents a journey of exploration.

Consequently, this approach requires greater program management skills and more resources compared to the platform or modular design approaches. A custom design strategy represents a high-risk approach for a potentially high reward. The reward should be high enough to compensate for the greater chance of failure. However, through the custom design strategy, an improved market position can be achieved and new business captured, which translates into greater revenue for the company.

Product development design strategy is not practiced through a singular, one-dimensional approach. Rather, selecting the appropriate strategy is influenced by several factors:

- The characteristics of the product itself
- The ability to leverage the existing product portfolio
- The expertise and knowledge of the company
- Customer and market trends

By using a strategy aligned with the characteristics of the product being developed, a company will be in position to

Characteristic	Design Strategy		
	Modular	Platform	Custom
Key Objective	Create new products through the utilization of preferred parts and modules	Create new products based on an existing baseline product	Create new products to expand the company product portfolio
Level of reuse	High	Medium	Low
Level of risk	Low	Medium	High
Level of resouce requirement and process discipline	Low	Medium	High
Key data elements and tools	• Product breakdown structure • Cataloged part data • Preferred parts and modules	• Technical require-ments flow-down matrix • Product experience domain • Component design compliance matrix	Leverage known data and tools as much as possible

Figure 9-9. Design Process Summary

make substantial gains in reducing product development cycle time and cost.

Selecting the appropriate design approach is critical for a company to develop a product in the most efficient way possible. Figure 9-9 shows a summary of the modular, platform, and custom design approaches. Built on the foundational elements, the design process initiates the building of the lean design pillar in the house of product development, as shown in Figure 9-10.

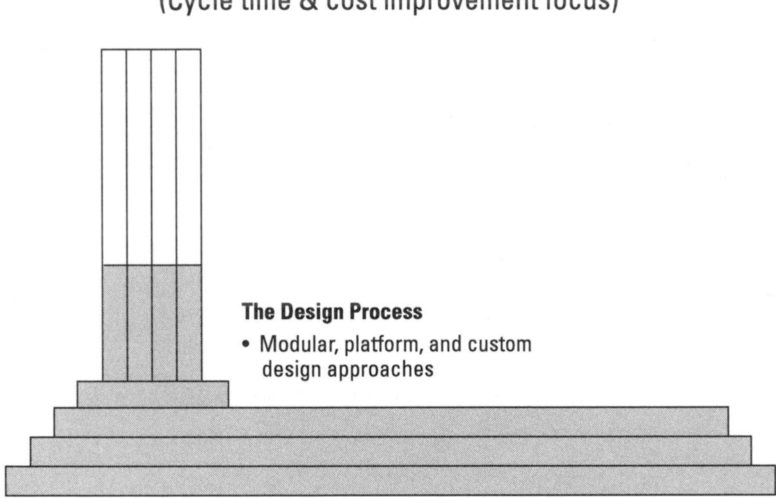

Figure 9-10. Building the Pillar of Lean Design

Proper application of the design strategies requires using vast amounts of product data. The ability to use this data efficiently and effectively is the premise behind "Chapter 10: Software Tools for Product Development."

CHAPTER 10

Software Tools for Product Development

As more and more part data is captured to support product development, through the reuse process introduced in Chapter 7 and the modular and platform design strategies highlighted in Chapter 9, the task of sifting through the data to find needed information becomes more difficult. For example, the spreadsheet format that was introduced in Chapter 7 is a convenient and simple way to catalog part attribute data through the reuse process, but it is not a user-friendly way to find specific information, especially for families that contain many parts. Figure 10-1 highlights some of these key data elements, identified in prior chapters, that support product development and aid in increasing the product knowledge of the company's product development practitioners.

From a user's perspective, the application of software tools in support of the product development process answers the following questions:

- How can I have quick and easy access to product data?
- How can I find a few key candidate parts with reuse potential from among an entire part family?
- How can I find specific data from among the numerous cataloged data elements?

Consequently, a key step to facilitate improvement in the product development process deals with the development of software tools that enable effective use of the available part data.

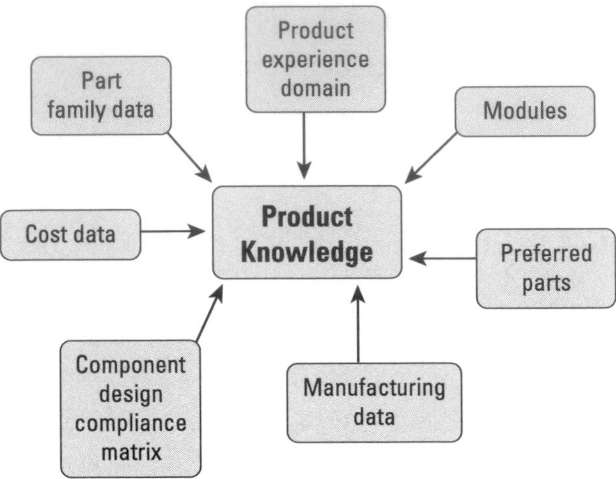

Figure 10-1. Data Elements for Product Development

THE SYSTEM ARCHITECTURE

As mentioned earlier, the need to acquire manufacturing and other business-related data in addition to engineering data is important to enable a comprehensive assessment of candidate parts with reuse potential. Consequently, a key feature of a product development database is one that links engineering part attribute data to these other data elements. Figure 10-2 illustrates system architecture that links part attribute data with other company information, which provides this comprehensive data set.

The approach here is to link the cataloged attribute data with the other data elements contained in a company's enterprise resource planning (ERP) and product data management (PDM) systems:

- An ERP system contains the information associated with the production side of a business. Specifically, information of this type includes customer order data, cost data, inventory/usage data, supplier and purchase data, and so on.

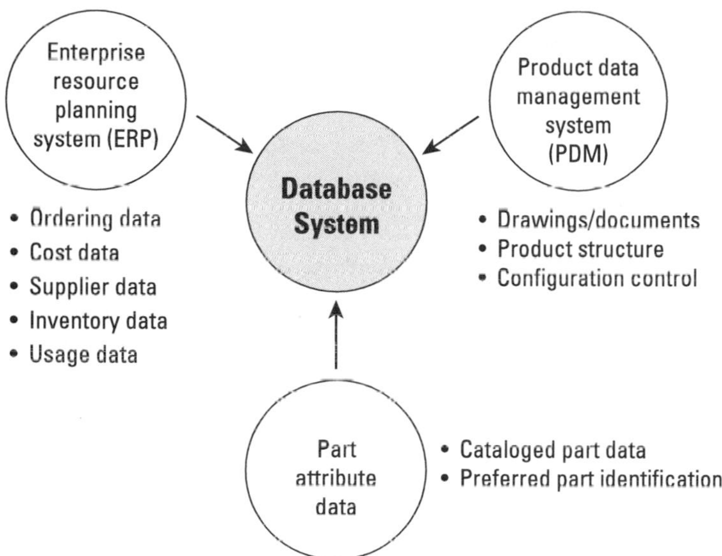

Figure 10-2. Database System Architecture

- In contrast, a PDM system collects, manages, and delivers product data.[1] Information of this type includes data that provides access to engineering drawings and other related documents, product data that describes a product's bill of material, and configuration control data that assesses the revision level status of each drawing and document.

Armed with this information, product development practitioners have the complete data package about the company's parts portfolio at their disposal, which enables them to make the right reuse decisions.

---

1. PDM systems are a logical place for storing part attribute data. For companies that employ PDM systems, the task of acquiring, storing, and maintaining attribute data may already be completed.

DATABASE DESIGN

Identifying part families and gathering attribute data is the cornerstone of the reuse process. Consequently, an integral part of a product development database is to enable easy access to this data.

As mentioned earlier concerning part attribute data, a myriad of different attributes may be identified for a particular part family. However, regarding the task of using attributes for selecting parts from among a whole family, it is not necessary to use all attributes for searching through part data. In most cases, only a subset of the identified attributes is required to aid in part searching. This subset represents the critical attributes that are instrumental in determining if a part has reuse potential. The balance of attributes helps to further differentiate specific parts in the family and narrow down those part candidates that have reuse potential. Software tools can be built to replicate this approach.

To illustrate this point, consider Company XYZ developing a product requiring the shaft component referenced earlier. Attributes that represent Company XYZ's shafts are shown in Figure 10-3.

Company XYZ Shaft Part Family Attributes

- Bearing Journal Diameter
- End Style Configuration
- Material
- Operating Temperature
- Part Number
- Cross-Hole Size
- Plating
- Shaft Length

Figure 10-3. Shaft Part Family Attributes

The eight attributes include dimensional parameters, material, and performance measures. However, in Company XYZ's case, only four of the eight attributes (i.e., bearing journal diameter, material, operating temperature, and shaft length) are necessary for part searching. The bearing journal diameter and shaft length are critical because they are the primary features that interface with mating parts. For example, the size of the journal diameter influences the selection of the mating bearing component that is used in the product. The operating temperature and material are also critical due to their influence on the operating environment and shaft wear characteristics.

These four attributes serve as the basis for creating a part searching software tool for Company XYZ's shaft components. An example search screen for a software tool of this nature is depicted in Figure 10-4.

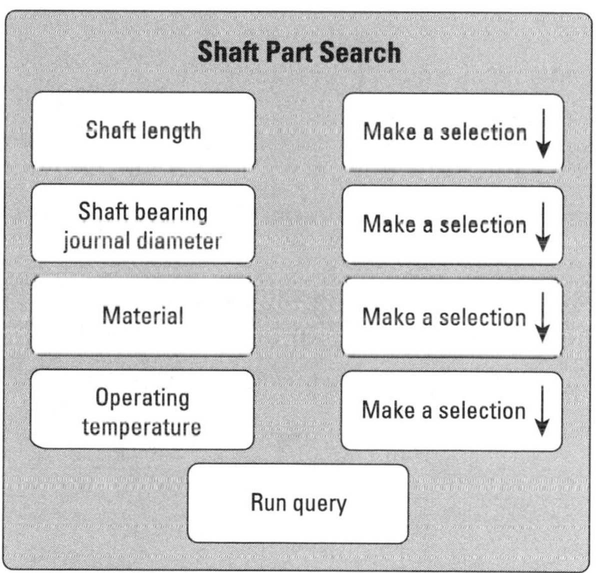

Figure 10-4. Software Tool Part Search Screen

The critical attributes are referenced in the left column. Associated with each attribute is a selection feature with a down arrow. Selecting the down arrow reveals a pull-down list that contains the specific data for each shaft attribute. The data list represents the collection of specific information for all parts represented by the shaft part family.

At this point, the user can make a selection from the available choices. In addition, the user has the option to repeat the procedure for each of the four attributes available for the shaft part family. Obviously, the more attributes that are selected, the more specific the search will be. Once the selections are made, the *Run query* button is selected to initiate the database search.

Shaft Part Search Report

Number of parts matching search criteria: 3

Part number	Preferred part	Material	Cross-hole size	Plating
S7-6238-1	yes [X] no [ ]	stainless steel	.250	chrome
Shaft length (min) (max)	**Bearing journal diameter** (min) (max)		**Operating temperature**	**End style configuration**
4.74 4.76	.8747 .8753		325° F	.125 x .75 slot

Part number	Preferred part	Material	Cross-hole size	Plating
S4-1937-6	yes [X] no [ ]	stainless steel	.250	chrome
Shaft length (min) (max)	**Bearing journal diameter** (min) (max)		**Operating temperature**	**End style configuration**
4.99 5.01	1.1257 1.1263		375° F	plain

Part number	Preferred part	Material	Cross-hole size	Plating
S7-5247-8	yes [ ] no [X]	aluminum	.3125	anodized
Shaft length (min) (max)	**Bearing journal diameter** (min) (max)		**Operating temperature**	**End style configuration**
4.49 4.51	.8747 .8753		200° F	plain

Figure 10-5. Part Search Report Example

The system responds with a report listing the specific shaft part numbers that match the user's selection criteria. In addition, the database provides not only the associated part attribute data for the four attributes listed on the system's search screen, but it also includes the part information for the balance of attributes in the report. An example of a part search report is shown in Figure 10-5.

MEASURING THE LEVEL OF REUSE

Because of the heavy reliance placed on preferred parts to support the implementation of a successful reuse strategy, it is often desirable for many companies to monitor how effectively the product development organization uses preferred parts in new product designs. To accomplish this, as a new product design is created, the list of individual parts needed to build the product, or, in other words, the product's bill of material (BOM), is assessed to determine the number of parts used in the product that are designated as preferred. Once this number is determined, an overall preferred parts utilization number can be calculated. This number (defined as the percentage of the number of preferred parts to the total number of parts used in the product) can be expressed in the following way:

$$\text{Preferred Parts Utilization} = \frac{\text{Number of Preferred Parts}}{\text{Total Number of Parts}}$$

For example, consider a bicycle company that employs a reuse process and wants to monitor the preferred parts utilization for its new bicycle designs. Figure 10-6 illustrates an example of a preferred parts utilization report that is generated as a result of performing a BOM assessment for a new bicycle design. As you can see, the bicycle's BOM contains a total of 15 parts, 10 of which are preferred parts. In this case, the preferred parts utilization is 67 percent (10/15).

Software tools provide an effective means for monitoring preferred parts utilization, and they eliminate the human element of performing a manual assessment. To accomplish this, the listing of preferred parts is preloaded into a database. For a new product requiring an assessment, the product's BOM is also loaded into the database. By prompting the system, the database performs a comparison of the product's BOM against the pre-loaded listing to identify preferred parts and calculates the

Product Bill of Material

Product: Bicycle

Part Description	Part Number	Quantity Required	Preferred Part
Wheel assembly	WH-12	2	Yes
Welded frame	AZ64P	1	No
Handle bar assembly	HB5	1	Yes
Seat assembly	ST-TY	1	No
Pedal	PD123	2	Yes
Chain	LK24	1	Yes
Brake assembly	BK143243	1	No
Reflector	RF-54	4	Yes
Seat bolt	B7H	1	No
Seat nut	N7H	1	No

Total parts: 15
Preferred Parts Utilization: 67%

Figure 10-6. Preferred Part Utilization Report

preferred parts utilization number. The database can also generate and print out a report similar to Figure 10-5.

Reports can be used in a variety of ways to monitor preferred parts utilization. For example, they can be used as supplemental data to support phase exit reviews (introduced in Chapter 8). Or, preferred part utilization numbers from individual reports can be rolled up to generate an overall utilization number that can be reported as part of a monthly metric.

In summary, experience has shown that sophisticated computer tools are unnecessary at the start of a reuse process implementation. Initially, developing simple and flexible software tools with an emphasis on maintaining current data has proven to be a highly successful approach. Later, as the reuse process implementation evolves and matures, the requirements of software tools will evolve and can be integrated accordingly. Coupled with the design process, this element further streamlines the product development process and builds on the lean design pillar in the house of product development (see Figure 10-7).

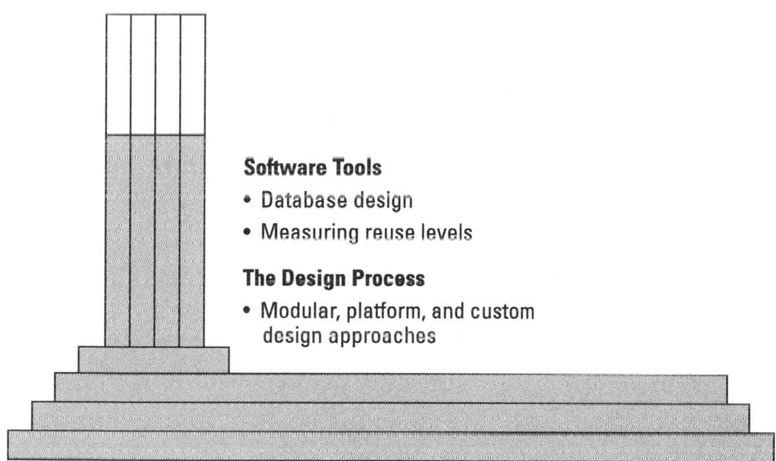

Figure 10-7. Building on the Lean Design Pillar

The ability to acquire the needed hardware for a product is equally important as the process for developing the product design. Consequently, a key element, and the next step for improvement is outlined in "Chapter 11: Integrating the Supply Chain in the Product Development Process."

CHAPTER 11

Integrating the Supply Chain in the Product Development Process

Up to this point, we've introduced several different concepts, including managing available resources to match workload, improving parts reuse, selecting the appropriate design strategy, and other ways to streamline a company's internal processes for designing and developing a product. If you recall from Chapter 2, the key goal of a lean business enterprise is to maximize value for the customer. In terms of product development, maximizing customer value means developing low-cost products and putting them in the hands of the customer in the shortest time possible. The strategies for improvement introduced in this book, so far, enable a company to reduce its own cycle time in developing a product design. These strategies, however, have minimal impact on reducing the cycle time and the cost of procuring hardware that is needed from suppliers in order to put the product in the customer's hands. For companies that rely heavily on their supply chain to provide parts for products they produce, this can be a major issue.

In many cases, the lead time for procuring parts from a supplier may exceed the company's time for designing the part. Due to the significance lead time plays in the overall product development value stream, in many cases a company cannot achieve its goals for product development unless it can reduce that lead time.

To illustrate this point, consider the case of the Tempo Thermostat Company shown in Figure 11-1. As you can see, Tempo's baseline product development cycle time ranged anywhere from 36 to 48 weeks, with an equal contribution of time associated with product development and supply chain activities. This cycle time included the time from when a project was kicked off to the delivery of the first unit of product to the customer. In terms of maximizing value, this was the true value stream.

Figure 11-1. Tempo Thermostat Company

Tempo's goal for product development was to put a new product in the hands of the customer in 12 weeks. However, in this case, the numbers speak for themselves. Even if Tempo was able to streamline its product development activities and reduce the cycle time essentially to zero, the company still would not be able to meet its overall goal for product development due to the time associated with the supply chain activities. Clearly, for Tempo to meet its goal, it will need to reduce the cycle time for manufacturing, procuring, and assembling its hardware.

A STRATEGY FOR IMPROVING THE SUPPLY CHAIN

For many companies operating under a traditional procurement process, when the product development organization completes an engineering blueprint drawing for a new part, it is "thrown over the wall" to the procurement organization, which selects a supplier for manufacturing the part from the company's supply base. Many factors influence the ultimate selection, including the identification of prospective suppliers, the buying agent selected for carrying out the procurement activity, the bids received for the particular part, and so on. As the procurement process is repeated for each new part purchased by the company, these factors, over time, contribute to the proliferation of the company's supply base. To illustrate this point, let's examine the supply base impact on the family of shaft components procured by Company XYZ.

Figure 11-2 is a pareto chart that shows the distribution of part numbers for different suppliers. In this case, the part numbers represent the entire part family of shaft components that Company XYZ produces. As you can see, only a few suppliers are predominant, while many other suppliers produce only a few parts. Of the 16 suppliers, 12 have 5 or fewer part numbers.

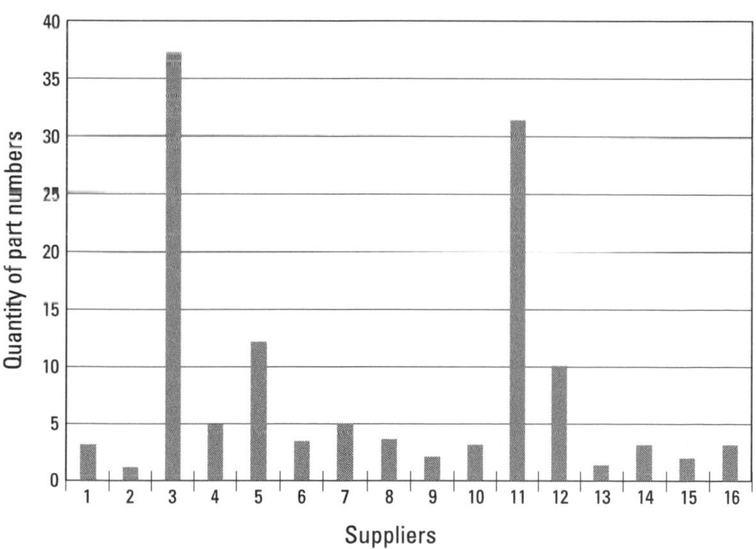

Figure 11-2. Analysis of Parts Purchased from Various Suppliers

Upon reviewing the data, several interesting questions come to mind:

- Does Company XYZ really need 16 different suppliers producing shaft components?
- What are the core competencies of the suppliers that manufacture only a few of the shaft part numbers?
- Does the supplier's level of expertise correlate with the lead time required for manufacturing shafts?
- Does Company XYZ truly get competitive pricing from suppliers that produce only a few part numbers in the family?

Hopefully, you can see that these questions raise several issues that can significantly influence a company's ability to meet its cycle time and cost goals for product development. In addition, the size of a company's supply base can also be an issue in terms of the overhead and management costs. Consequently, a key element of a company's supply chain strategy is to minimize the size of its supply base.

As shown by the shaft example, reviewing the distribution of part numbers and suppliers from the perspective of a part family is very enlightening. Clearly, Company XYZ does not need 16 different suppliers producing shaft components. As a result, profiling a company's supply base from the perspective of a part family exposes opportunities for consolidation and improvement. Consequently, the same part families that are developed to support improvements in product development can also be leveraged as the basis for formulating a supply chain strategy. This strategy is presented in Figure 11-3.

As you can see, the philosophy of reducing product variation by using part families and preferred parts in product development is extended to include the company's supply base. The goal here is to reduce the supply base by eliminating non-preferred suppliers. Further, this is facilitated by aligning part fam-

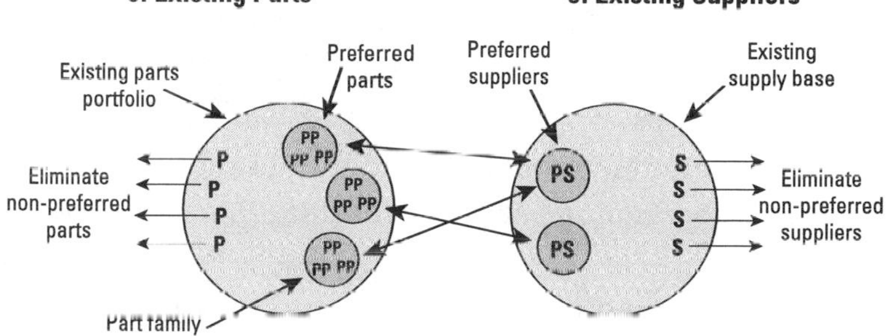

Figure 11-3. Supply Chain Strategy to Reduce Procurement Cost and Time

ilies with preferred suppliers, based on requirements that match the characteristics of the parts with each supplier's capabilities.

Together, the design and manufacturing requirements unique to each part determine the procurement cost and lead time. From a supplier's perspective, the approach of grouping these requirements based on part families has a significant impact in terms of standardizing work processes, simplifying inspection requirements, reducing set-up times, and so on. Leveraged against a family of common parts, these factors provide economies of scale that can significantly reduce part cost and lead time.

PROCURING PART FAMILIES VS. INDIVIDUAL PARTS

As just described, part families provide an effective means and the foundation for reducing procurement lead time and part cost within a company's supply chain. Also, the key element of this strategy is to align preferred suppliers with part families based on design and manufacturing requirements. So, based on this, is it simply a matter of selecting a preferred supplier for each part family? Realistically speaking, probably not. Within a part family, the design and manufacturing requirements are often too broad to maximize the cost and lead time benefits. In these cases, it is necessary to break the family down into smaller pieces to better align parts with the appropriate suppliers. To illustrate this, let's go back to the shaft example of Company XYZ.

All of Company XYZ's shafts essentially fall into one of three different configurations. In addition, the shafts are produced, basically, from two different materials: Material A for high vibration applications, and Material B for low vibration applications. The different configurations and material of the shaft components are needed to meet certain design requirements, but these variables have significant manufacturing implications as well. Material A is much more difficult to machine than Material B, and the configuration of the part influences the manufacturing sequence and process steps, the machines used to manufacture the parts, and even possibly, the tooling. By reviewing the family of shafts, based on these variables, it's possible to break the family down into logical pieces that better support the supply chain strategy. This is illustrated with the tree diagram shown in Figure 11-4.

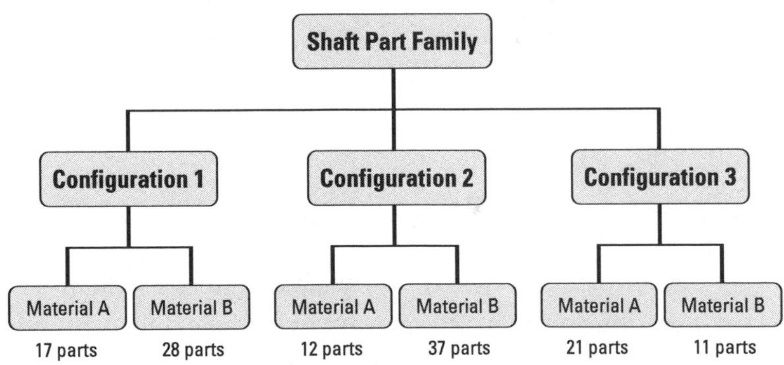

Figure 11-4. Shaft Part Family Subgroups

Notice the similarity in format between Figure 11-4 and the product breakdown structure introduced earlier in Chapter 9 (Figure 9-3, page 122). Both employ a tree diagram, but with different objectives. With the product breakdown structure, the goal was to identify opportunities for modules and the reuse of parts. Here, the goal is to break a part family down into logical pieces to support the supply chain strategy.

As you can see in Figure 11-4, six subgroups are created, based on the combination of configuration and material. The numbers below the material blocks on the bottom of the tree are the quantities of parts numbers within each subgroup of shafts. Following this analysis, the procurement organization would be engaged to transition the parts within the subgroups to the preferred suppliers. When the parts are transitioned, they are placed with the selected suppliers, subgroup by subgroup. In other words, all of the parts within a specific subgroup are placed with one supplier and not divided among multiple suppliers. This approach provides the greatest leverage for the supplier, which, in turn, results in the greatest cost benefit for the company—a true partnering relationship!

In terms of cycle time, by identifying pre-selected suppliers using the part family approach, a company virtually eliminates the need to canvass the supply base to find a supplier for a newly created part. In other words, as new parts are created by the product development organization, they are automatically placed with the designated supplier for the particular part family. With this new approach, the only remaining activity is to negotiate a price for the new component with the supplier. And even this is somewhat simplified, because the quoted price for the new component can be leveraged against other parts in the grouping produced by the supplier to ensure a measure of consistency. By eliminating a quote-and-bid process that could take weeks for the company's procurement organization, cycle time is reduced.

In addition, the part family strategy promotes the philosophy of *concurrent engineering*. For example, if a designer creating a new part has questions about the component's manufacturing impact on the product design, he or she can contact the pre-selected supplier for the part, early in the development process, and work to resolve the issues.

In summary, a part family approach helps to bridge the gap between the product development and supply chain organizations. Several engineering and manufacturing factors can influence the breakdown of a part family: size, function, configuration, key physical features, material, tooling, manufacturing approach, and others. By considering these factors from the perspective of the supplier, and by aligning the parts by family, a company can substantially reduce its procurement lead time and the cost of the parts it procures.

IMPLEMENTING A VALUE-ENGINEERING PROGRAM

In addition to the benefits already discussed, the part family approach also sets the stage for implementing a value-engineering program with a parts manufacturer. A value-engineering program is essentially a collaborative effort between a company and its parts provider with the goal of reducing cost for their mutual benefit. In one successful example, a company and its supplier worked together to generate ideas that resulted in design modifications for parts, which reduced the manufacturing cost for the supplier and, in turn, the purchase cost for the company.

By leveraging cost and usage data for parts comprising a family, a company can identify the best candidates for cost-reduction opportunities. For example, consider data from a subgroup of shaft components from Company XYZ depicted in Figure 11-5. Each dot represents a different part number within the subgroup; the scatter is based on the projected usage requirements of each part and the unit cost. Because we are considering a family of parts with similar characteristics, in other words comparing apples to apples, it's very easy to iden-

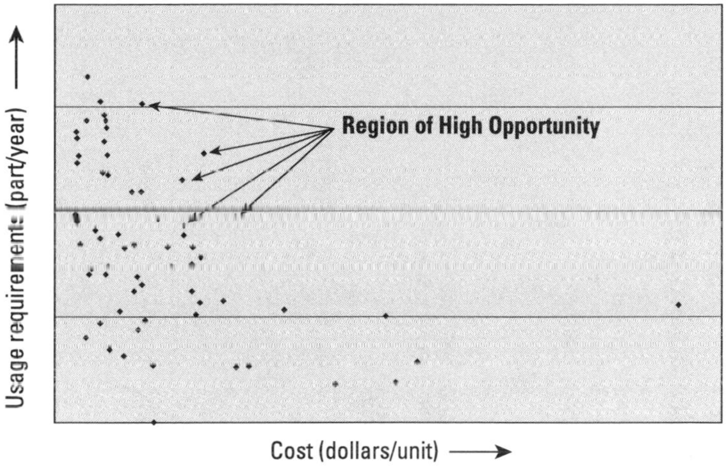

Figure 11-5. Subgroup Analysis for Value Engineering

tify high volume, high cost parts, which represent the best opportunity for cost reduction.

By performing an analysis similar to Figure 11-5, a company can identify which parts have the most potential for maximizing the benefit for the company and its parts provider, which therefore results in an extremely efficient and effective value-engineering program. In addition, based on a part family approach, suppliers can leverage cost-reduction improvements identified from an individual part across the representative family of parts they produce, to realize additional benefits.

Integrating the supply chain with the product development process is necessary to meet the overall goals of reduced cycle time and cost. Figure11-6 is a summary of the supplier and parts reduction strategy. Due to the heavy role that suppliers play in terms of a company's value stream, the supply chain is a key contributor in maximizing customer value. This element completes the lean design pillar in the house of product development, as shown in Figure 11-7.

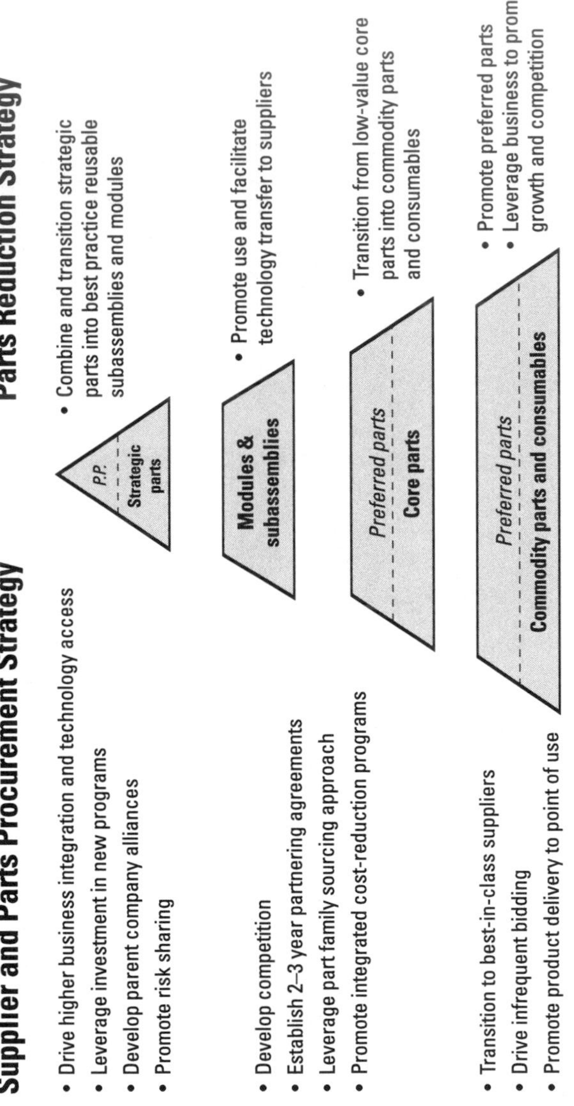

Figure 11-6. Supplier and Parts Procurement/Reduction Strategy

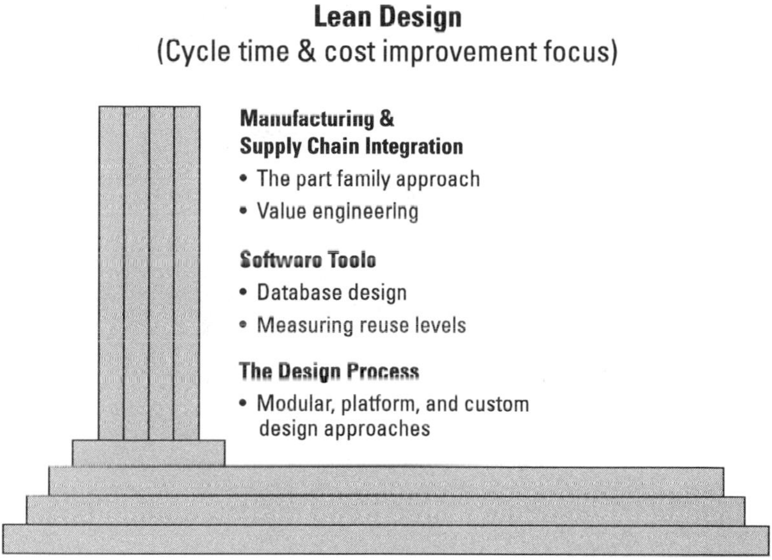

Lean Design
(Cycle time & cost improvement focus)

Manufacturing &
Supply Chain Integration
- The part family approach
- Value engineering

Software Tools
- Database design
- Measuring reuse levels

The Design Process
- Modular, platform, and custom design approaches

Figure 11-7. Completing the Lean Design Pillar

This chapter completes Part Four of this book, which addressed elements to improve cycle time and cost aspects of product development. Part Five addresses the topic of improving quality in the product development process and begins with "Chapter 12: Instituting a Manufacturing Process Control Program."

PART FIVE

Quality in the Product Development Process

Part Five describes elements that improve product quality through the product development process: implementing manufacturing process control and design for six sigma. It concludes with a look at flow and cell design.

CHAPTER 12

Instituting a Manufacturing Process Control Program

Up to now, the lean concepts and tools discussed have focused heavily on reducing cycle time and cost. However, another key element, quality, is critical to achieving the goal of maximizing customer value related to product development. If you will remember Figure 1-3 (reproduced here as Figure 12-1), different tactical objectives and tools are required in order to improve quality. These objectives are focused primarily on variation reduction and process control.

Collectively, *Manufacturing Process Control* and Design for Six Sigma (discussed in Chapter 13) address the issue of improving product quality through the development process. Implementing these elements help answer the following questions:

- Can the product be manufactured or assembled without any problems?
- Does the product perform in accordance with the customer's specification?
- Will the product meet the customer's expectation in terms of product reliability and durability?

WHAT IS MANUFACTURING PROCESS CONTROL?

Let's begin with an explanation of Manufacturing Process Control (MPC). MPC is a disciplined approach for assessing the variability of part features by analyzing measurement data derived during inspection of those features. The goal of minimizing

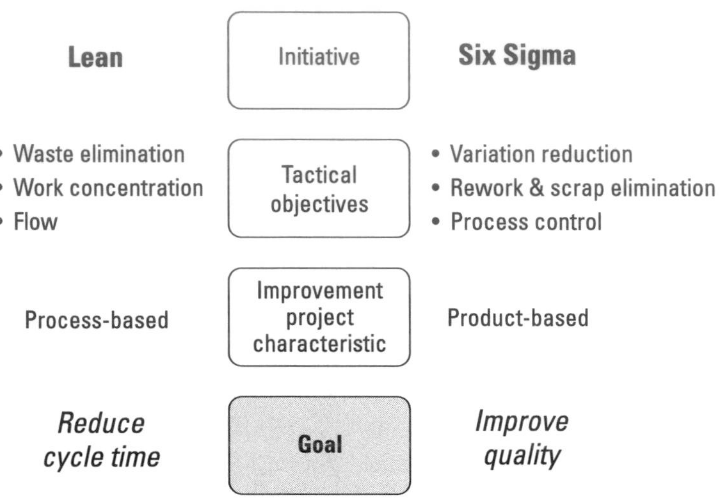

Figure 12-1. Lean and Six Sigma

variability is accomplished by controlling the process parameters that influence the manufacture of the part features. Based on this, MPC is most effective when it is implemented across a family of common parts with similar characteristics. Consequently, the same part families that are created for product development and leveraged in developing a supply chain strategy can also be used to improve product quality through MPC. The objectives of implementing manufacturing process control are to:

- Reduce variation on critical part features
- Reduce scrap and rework cost
- Develop a consistent method to turn specific part number actions into systemic improvement
- Capture part data to support the creation of process capability models that feed Design for Six Sigma

IMPLEMENTING AN MPC PROGRAM

The steps for implementing an MPC program are provided in Figure 12-2 and described in more detail in the following sections.

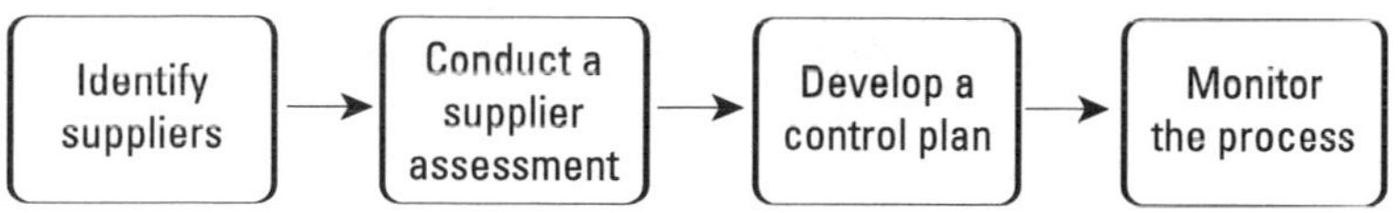

Figure 12-2. MPC Implementation Process

Step 1: Identify Suppliers

To clarify, a company should also implement an MPC program within its internal manufacturing facility. However, since many companies rely heavily on their supply base for manufacturing parts, Figures 12-2 and 12-3 are presented in the context of implementing an MPC program with suppliers.

Supplier Selection Matrix

Supplier	Supplier Strategy	MPC Commitment	Supplier's Quality System
Supplier A	Growth	Yes	Excellent
Supplier B	New program	Yes	Adequate
Supplier C	Critical part families	Yes	Excellent
Supplier D	Growth & transitions	Yes	Excellent
Supplier E	Maintain	No	Poor
Supplier F	Maintain	No	Adequate
Supplier G	Phase out	No	Poor

Yes
No

Engineering-driven issues
- New product introduction

Procurement-driven issues
- Growth of supplier
- Part family transition

Quality-driven issues
- Chronic quality-problem parts

Figure 12-3. MPC Supplier Selection

The selection of suitable suppliers for MPC implementation can be influenced by several different factors. As shown in Figure 12-3, these factors extend beyond quality-related issues. In addition, the company should also consider the capabilities of candidate suppliers in implementing a successful MPC program.

Part Number	Manufacturing Process Step															
	Pull Raw Material	Machine Operation 1	Machine Operation 2	Machine Operation 3	Machine Operation 4	Machine Operation 5	Machine Operation 6	Clean Operation 1	Clean Operation 2	Plating Operation 1	Plating Operation 2	Finish Operation 1	Assembly Operation 1	Assembly Operation 2	Identification Operation	Storage
Part 1	X	X	X		X			X				X	X		X	X
Part 2	X	X	X		X	X		X				X			X	X
Part 3	X	X	X		X			X				X			X	X
Part 4	X	X	X		X			X				X			X	X
Part 5	X	X	X	X	X	X	X	X	X	X	X	X	X	X	X	X
Part 6	X	X	X		X			X				X	X		X	X
Part 7	X	X	X		X			X		X					X	X
Part 8	X	X	X		X	X		X	X	X					X	X
Part 9	X	X	X		X			X				X			X	X
Part 10	X	X	X		X	X	X	X				X			X	X
Part 11	X	X	X	X	X			X					X		X	X
Part 12	X	X	X		X			X	X	X		X			X	X
Part 13	X	X	X		X	X	X	X		X		X			X	X
Part 14	X	X	X		X			X				X	X		X	X
Part 15	X	X	X		X			X	X			X			X	X
Part 16	X	X	X	X	X	X	X	X		X					X	X
Part 17	X	X	X		X	X		X				X	X		X	X
Part 18	X	X	X		X			X				X			X	X
Part 19	X	X	X		X	X		X				X	X		X	X
Part 20	X	X	X		X			X				X			X	X

Figure 12-4. Part Number and Process Matrix

Two key elements that influence the success of a supplier implementing MPC are the capability of the supplier's quality system and the level of management team support.

Step 2: Conduct a Supplier Assessment

As stated previously, the benefits of MPC are maximized when leveraged against a part family. A tool to assist suppliers in assessing a family of parts is known as a *part number and process matrix*, shown in Figure 12-4. The purpose in using the matrix is to help suppliers answer key questions regarding the parts they manufacture, such as:

- What critical process steps are used in the manufacture of our parts?
- What key part features drive the quality of our parts?
- What key factors influence cost?

Specifically, the purpose of the part number and process matrix is to assess the manufacturing steps for each part across the entire part family and to determine the level of commonality. Incidentally, the application of this matrix represents another example of employing the concept of group technology.

By completing the matrix, the predominant operations necessary to manufacture the parts in the family will become readily apparent. Armed with this information, a company can take action to ensure that its manufacturing processes, among all parts, are standardized as much as possible. In addition, the company can use the information derived from the part number and process matrix to create a manufacturing cell for producing the parts in the family. By understanding the key manufacturing processes for the parts from the matrix, the company can arrange the required machines and manufacturing equipment in a sequential fashion, as shown in Figure 12-5, to create a lean cell.[1] The cellular design approach is a key enabler to facilitate waste elimination and establish flow in the factory.

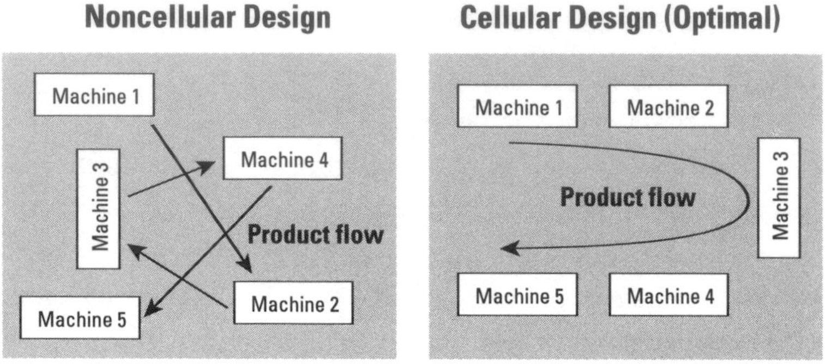

Noncellular Design **Cellular Design (Optimal)**

Figure 12-5. Comparison of Factory Layouts

Step 3: Develop a Control Plan

A control plan is a tool that helps manage critical process inputs to ensure that a process continually meets its product or service goals. Related to MPC, a control plan is intended to control the inputs in the manufacturing processes that affect the variation of key part features, otherwise known as *key characteristics*. The control plan contains elements to determine what to control, the detection method, the measurement frequency, and appropriate actions to take. An example of a control plan form is illustrated in Figure 12-6.

Step 4: Monitor the Process

Step 4 is the critical step that requires the supplier to possess a quality system capable of supporting an MPC program. For example, the supplier should have some form of data repository for storing and retrieving part inspection data, as well as resources with expertise that are capable of assessing the data using analysis tools. In addition, this step represents activities

1. Note: Implementation of the part family strategy outlined in Chapter 11 provides the catalyst and incentive for suppliers to implement a cellular design approach to facilitate manufacturing.

<table>
<tr><th colspan="11">Manufacturing Process Control Plan</th></tr>
<tr><td colspan="4">Control plan number:</td><td colspan="3">Supplier/site:</td><td colspan="3">Supplier number:</td><td>Date:</td></tr>
<tr><td colspan="5">Product line:</td><td colspan="6">Part family:</td></tr>
<tr><td colspan="3">Part number:</td><td colspan="5">Part description:</td><td colspan="2">☐ Production</td><td>☐ Development</td></tr>
<tr><td colspan="4">Process owner:</td><td colspan="3">Approval:</td><td colspan="4">Preparer:</td></tr>
<tr><td rowspan="2">Operation number</td><td rowspan="2">Operation Description</td><td rowspan="2">Equipment/ load center</td><td colspan="2">Key characteristics</td><td colspan="5">Methods</td><td rowspan="2">Reaction plan</td></tr>
<tr><td>Input</td><td>Output</td><td>Product tolerance/ process spec</td><td>Measurement technique</td><td>Sample size</td><td>Sample frequency</td><td>Control method</td></tr>
<tr><td></td><td></td><td></td><td></td><td></td><td></td><td></td><td></td><td></td><td></td><td></td></tr>
<tr><td></td><td></td><td></td><td></td><td></td><td></td><td></td><td></td><td></td><td></td><td></td></tr>
<tr><td></td><td></td><td></td><td></td><td></td><td></td><td></td><td></td><td></td><td></td><td></td></tr>
<tr><td></td><td></td><td></td><td></td><td></td><td></td><td></td><td></td><td></td><td></td><td></td></tr>
</table>

Figure 12-6. Control Plan Form

that ensure adherence to the control plan. More specifically, this step includes providing information in the form of feedback to the product development organization regarding adherence to key characteristics that engineering generates.

THE ROLE OF KEY CHARACTERISTICS

Key characteristics are individual features of a part whose variation has significant influence on product fit, performance, reliability, or manufacturing. Key characteristics play an important role in the implementation of an MPC program. Specifically, key characteristics serve three objectives regarding MPC implementation. They:

- Identify the key features that require data collection through the MPC program.
- Identify the individual part features whose variation affects the overall product.
- Facilitate communication between the product development and manufacturing disciplines.

The product development or engineering organization identifies part features whose variation affects the overall product fit, performance, and reliability. Conversely, the part supplier or manufacturing entity identifies part features whose variation influences manufacturing.

To illustrate the concept of key characteristics, consider the example in Figure 12-7. Let's assume this crude illustration of a

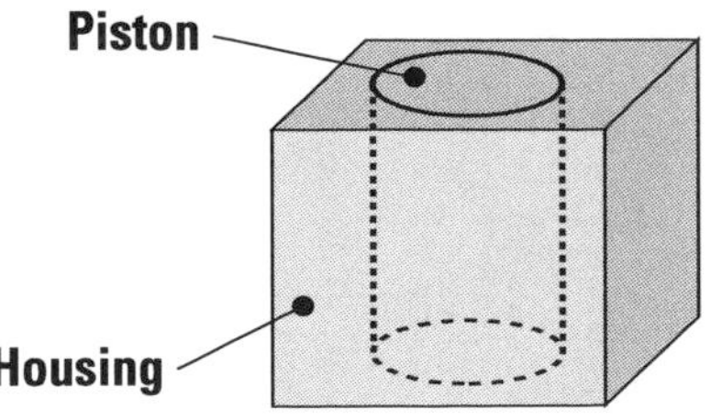

Figure 12-7. Product Example of a Housing and Piston

housing and piston represents a product produced by a company. Let's also assume that the customer has indicated that leakage between the piston and the housing is the critical performance parameter for this product. This leakage requirement is known as a *critical-to-quality* (CTQ) characteristic. A CTQ is defined as one of the select few characteristics of a product that has a significant impact on product performance or customer satisfaction.

In this example, the role of key characteristics is to identify the individual part features of the housing and piston whose variation has a significant influence on the leakage requirement. Referring to Figure 12-8, we see a cross-sectioned view of the housing and piston assembly illustrating the leakage path. Also in the figure, we see that the inside diameter of the housing and the outside diameter of the piston are identified as the key characteristics. In other words, the variability of the inside diameter of the housing coupled with the variability of the outside diameter of the piston influence the leakage level for this product. Regarding MPC, the goal is to implement controls in the manufacturing process that minimize the variability in producing these features. The targeted values for the specific sizes for producing these features are determined by the

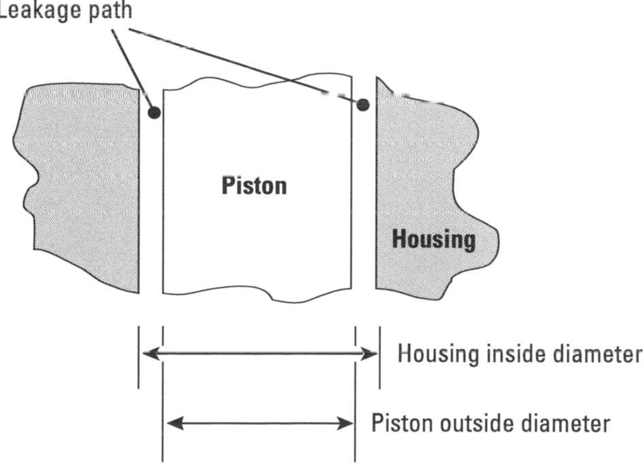

Figure 12-8. Product Cross Section Identifying Key Characteristics

product development organization and communicated through the engineering drawing package for these parts.

Several tools that can be used to help identify key characteristics based on customer CTQ's include cause-and-effect diagrams, quality function deployment (QFD), and failure mode and effects analysis (FMEA), among others. These tools represent transfer functions that identify the relationship between part features and customer requirements.

Manufacturing Process Control helps improve product quality. By integrating the MPC approach into the supply chain as well as captive manufacturing facilities, companies can make great strides in reducing cost, and curtail activities associated with fixing quality-related problems. Regarding the house of product development, MPC implementation represents the starting point for building the quality pillar, as shown in Figure 12-9.

Quality Design
(Quality improvement focus)

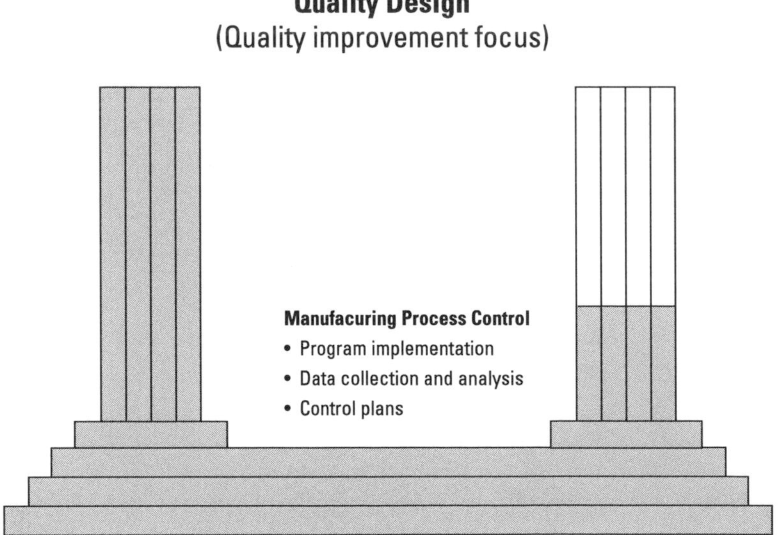

Figure 12-9. Building the Quality Pillar

Once a company has implemented MPC successfully, it can focus on the next level of product quality, which is discussed in "Chapter 13: Implementing Design for Six Sigma."

CHAPTER 13

Implementing Design for Six Sigma

Design for Six Sigma (DFSS) represents the second topic related to improving product quality through product development. As the words "design for" imply, DFSS strives to proactively improve quality by preventing defects and reducing variation during the design phase of developing products. Consequently, the key objectives of Design for Six Sigma are:

- Predict the quality level of new product designs
- Design quality into new products
- Improve the quality of existing products

THE MEANING OF SIGMA

The term *sigma* (symbolically represented by the Greek letter of the same name [σ]) refers to standard deviation, which is a measure of the variation or scatter in a process. Within business and industry, the sigma value is a metric that indicates how well a process is performing, compared to the benchmark value of six sigma (6σ). Sigma measures the capability of a process to perform defect-free work. A defect is anything that may result in customer dissatisfaction.

The common measurement for six sigma is defects per unit, where a unit can be virtually anything: a component, an administrative form, a piece of material, a line of software code, and so on. The sigma value is a quality measurement that indicates how often a defect is likely to occur. The higher the sigma value, the less likely a process will produce defects. As sigma increases, cycle time and cost decreases, and customer satisfaction increases.

So what does it mean to be six sigma? Consider a process that produces one million parts. A six sigma process is one that produces less than four defective parts out of the million that are produced![1] Clearly, achieving a six sigma quality level represents world-class status.

THE IMPORTANCE OF DESIGN FOR SIX SIGMA

Variation of nearly all data can be graphically represented in terms of the normal distribution or bell-shaped curve, an example of which is shown in Figure 13-1. The mean, or average, of the distribution is represented by the Greek letter mu (μ). The sigma level of a process is the number of standard deviations between the mean of the process and the closest specification limit. Figure 13-1 shows a six sigma process.

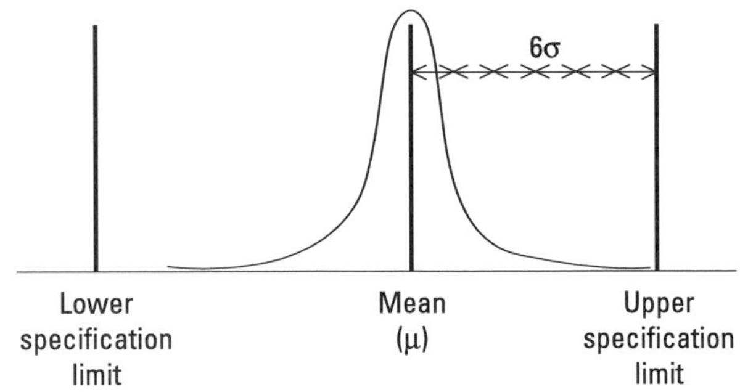

Figure 13-1. Graphical Representation of a Six Sigma Process

The actual sigma score compares the "voice of a process" to the "voice of the customer." To clarify, the "voice of a process" is

1. The exact number of a six sigma process is one that produces only 3.4 defects per million opportunities.

the inherent variation within a process. It is represented by the bell-shaped curve and distributed about the mean. The "voice of the customer" is represented by the specification limits that are ultimately related to meeting a customer requirement, which is represented in Figure 13-2. The sigma score, defined by the capitol letter Z, is a measurement that compares the output of the process with the customer requirement (the specification limit). As you can see, the portion of the distribution that falls beyond the specification limit represents defects.

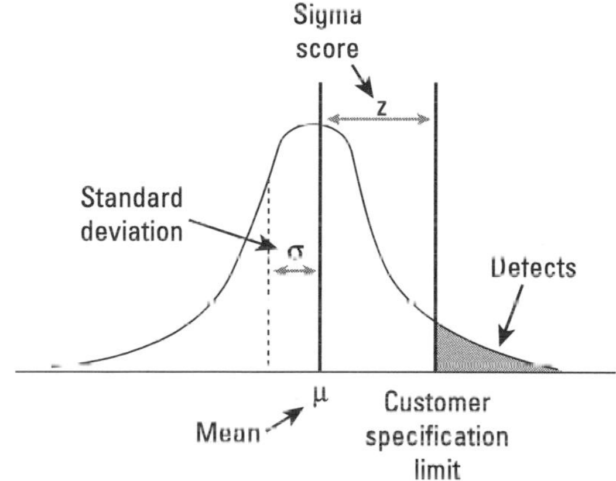

Figure 13-2. Impact of the Sigma Score

Companies employing DFSS seek to reduce variation. In terms of the bell curve, this is represented by the curve's slope. The steeper the slope, the lower the level of variation. This is illustrated in Figure 13-3 by the bell-shaped curves for the traditional product and DFSS product.

DFSS is intended to reduce the inherent variation in a product's design in order to achieve a competitive advantage. In addition, DFSS helps to transform the product development process in the following ways:

- From a process of evolving design requirements to disciplined requirements flow down and management

- Where design by testing is replaced with design by analysis
- Where extensive design rework is eliminated by identifying and controlling key design parameters
- From a condition where performance, manufacturing, and reliability problems are fixed in the production phase to one that anticipates and eliminates problems prior to the release of the design

In summary, Design for Six Sigma is the catalyst in moving the product development process from a condition where design quality is reactive to a state where design quality is predictive.

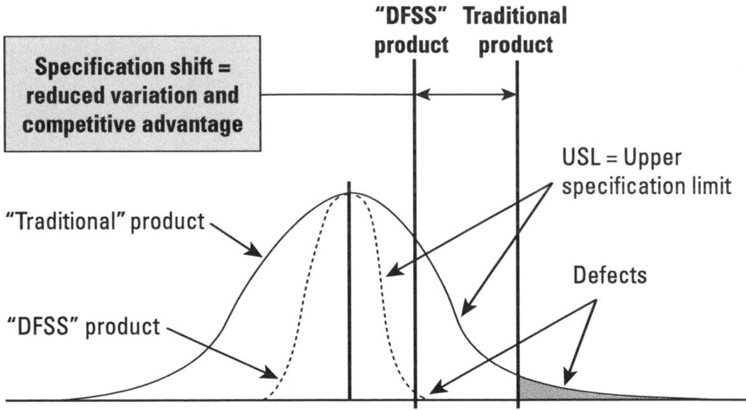

Figure 13-3. Impact of Design for Six Sigma

THE ELEMENTS OF DESIGN FOR SIX SIGMA

As noted earlier, a six sigma product is one that contains only 3.4 defective products for every million products that are produced. A defect could be virtually anything that has an impact on customer satisfaction. Therefore, with respect to defects in products, defects can occur in all levels in a product's value stream ranging from the procurement of raw material needed to manufacture an individual component to the wear-out characteristics of the end-unit product. Based on this broad spectrum of potential sources of defects, the elements of design for six sigma can be summarized into three key areas illustrated in Figure 13-4.

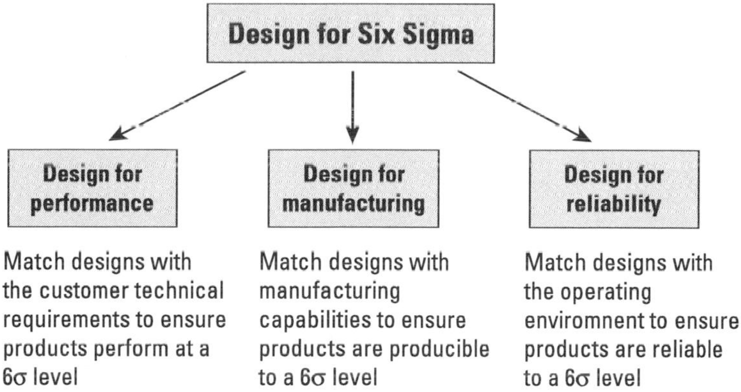

Figure 13-4. Elements of Design for Six Sigma

Let's take a look at each area in closer detail.

Design for Performance

This assesses a product's performance based on the measurement of product test data. It essentially measures the product's performance against the customer's technical requirements. Performance can be assessed for end-unit products, assemblies, and modules, but not individual components, because they do not perform.

Design for Manufacturing

This assesses a product's manufacturing capability based on the measurement of inspection data of an individual component. Inspection data derived from manufacturing process control (discussed in Chapter 12) are enablers for completing a design for manufacturing assessment.

Design for Reliability

This assesses a product's reliability based on an analysis of warranty data and company escapes. Warranty data focuses on determining product wear-out characteristics and life-cycle requirements. Company escapes focus on addressing product quality issues that escape through the company's quality control system, and are identified by the customer. These may involve design-related modifications.

Utilizing DFSS, a company can measure the sigma value of its product elements by using a *product scorecard*. This tool determines the sigma score (quality level) of a product's capability in terms of its performance, manufacturing capability, and reliability. Using statistics, the scorecard provides a concise summary of the quality level of the product and adds the following benefits:

- It identifies areas of improvement for existing products based on low sigma scores.
- It predicts the quality level of new products by using existing sigma scores and data from similar products.
- It helps the company prioritize what process and product improvement it wants to focus on.

Figure 13-5 shows the components of a sample product scorecard. As you can see, a separate scorecard is generated for each DFSS element (i.e., performance, manufacturing, and reliability). However, each element uses the same basic format (as shown with the scorecard template depicted at the bottom of Figure 13-5).

On a performance scorecard, each row corresponds to a different test performed for a product. If a product requires six tests to be performed, the scorecard contains six individual entries with sigma scores calculated for each individual test. The individual sigma scores are then rolled up to determine an overall value representing the performance sigma score. This is entered on the product scorecard summary shown at the top of Figure 13-5.

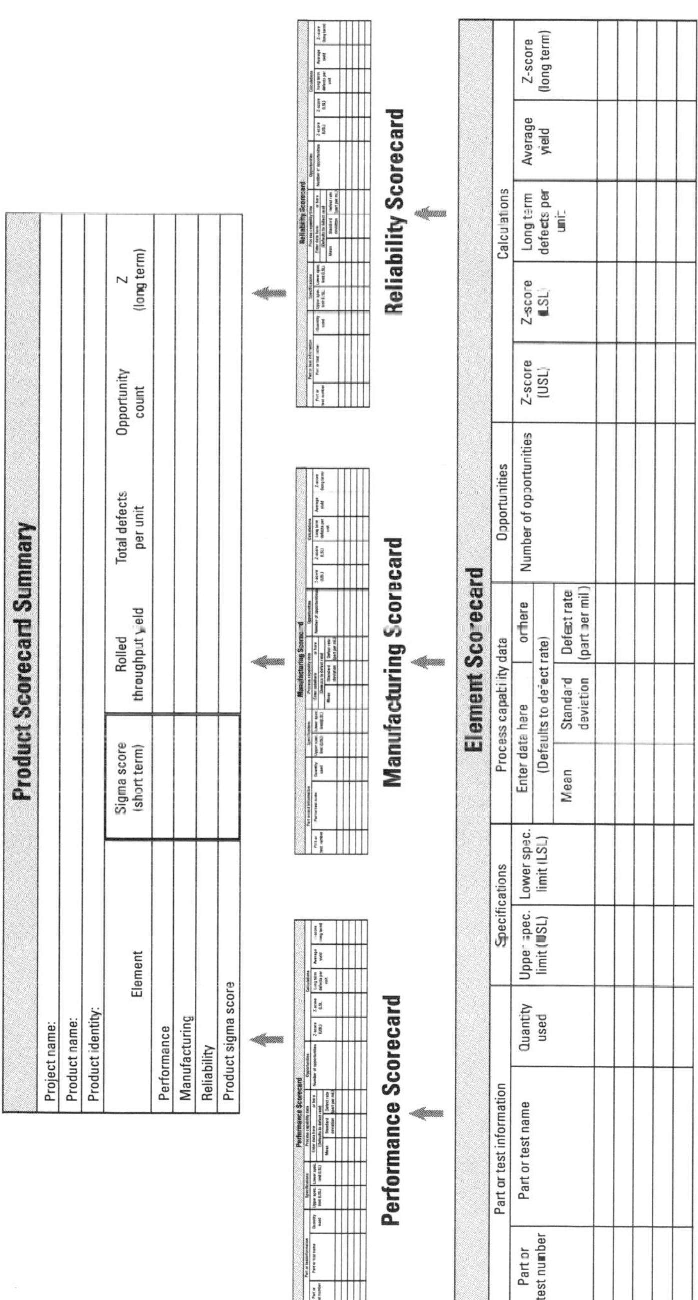

Figure 13-5. Product Scorecard Structure

On a manufacturing scorecard, each row corresponds to a different individual component required by the end product. Consequently, the entire list of individual components, or, in other words, the product's bill of material, can be designated using this approach. The collective sigma score from the individual components is calculated, representing the manufacturing sigma score, and is then entered on the product scorecard summary.

Reliability scorecards use this same approach. The aggregate reliability value, representing the reliability sigma score of the product, is also entered on the product scorecard summary. Once a company determines its sigma values for each of the three DFSS elements, it can roll these up to derive a product sigma score for the product. The product sigma score represents the overall quality level of the product related to its performance, manufacturing capability, and reliability.

IMPLEMENTING DESIGN FOR SIX SIGMA

The process for implementing design for six sigma can be summarized in four key steps, shown in Figure 13-6. Successful implementation of DFSS requires that this approach be integrated and used throughout the product development process.

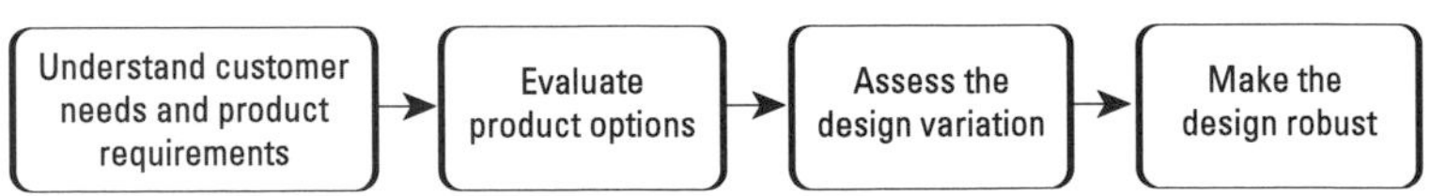

Figure 13-6. Design for Six Sigma Implementation Process

Step 1: Understand Customer Needs and Product Requirements

Essentially, this entails determining the requirements that define product success or failure in the eyes of the customer. Recalling the discussion of MPC in Chapter 12, these requirements are referred to as critical-to-quality (CTQ) characteristics.

Developing a thorough understanding of customer needs and CTQs are critical ingredients in maximizing customer value. It may require the company that is tasked with developing the product to take the initiative and engage the customer in a dialog to acquire the necessary information. Experience has shown that the straightforward approach of simply talking to customers is an excellent way to gain a true understanding of their needs.

Step 2: Evaluate Product Options

To accomplish this, it is imperative that a company identifies the primary variables that drive the design. Once a company has determined the variables, it can use this information to develop a solution that meets the customer needs. One of the more popular tools to help assess customer and product requirements is quality function deployment, or QFD. If you recall, QFDs were briefly mentioned in Chapter 12. Quality function deployment is a detailed system for translating the needs and wishes of the customer into design requirements for products and services. The tool allows a company to prioritize and assess customer needs against functional product requirements, so that the company can generate an aggregate score and understand the relative importance of each requirement.

Step 3: Assess the Design Variation

This step involves determining the individual key characteristics and assessing the variation that drives CTQs. In many instances, analytical models can be developed and used to aid in assessing variation and understanding the relationship between the requirements and CTQs. In addition, this step includes determining the probability of failure in meeting a customer requirement and the development of risk mitigation plans.

Step 4: Make the Design Robust

This step uses trade-off studies to facilitate and balance the effects of product performance, customer requirements, and cost. From a manufacturing perspective, the ability to determine the appropriate tolerance for a part feature is predicated on a company understanding the trade-off between the cost and capability of the manufacturing process to produce the feature, using process capability models.

USING PROCESS CAPABILITY MODELS

A *process capability model* is an analytical tool that uses historical data to predict the sigma value for a part feature based on the specific manufacturing process used to produce the feature. A part feature may be a hole, surface, cutout, or any other physical characteristic of a part. The sigma value determined by the model is based not only on the particular manufacturing process but also by other factors that influence the process such as the material type, size of the feature, tolerance, and cut distance.

The historical data needed to create process capability models comes from the data generated from implementing a Manufacturing Process Control program. Consequently, MPC implementation is the logical precursor to DFSS implementation.

However, in cases where an MPC program has not been established and data is not available, commercially available tools are available that contain a library of canned process capability models. For companies initiating a DFSS program, these commercial tools provide the benefit of jump-starting the implementation by saving time and effort in generating part data. The data, used by these tools to create models, is based on common manufacturing processes used throughout industry. However, these tools are readily adaptable and provide companies with flexibility to add additional processes and data that may be unique to a particular industry or business.

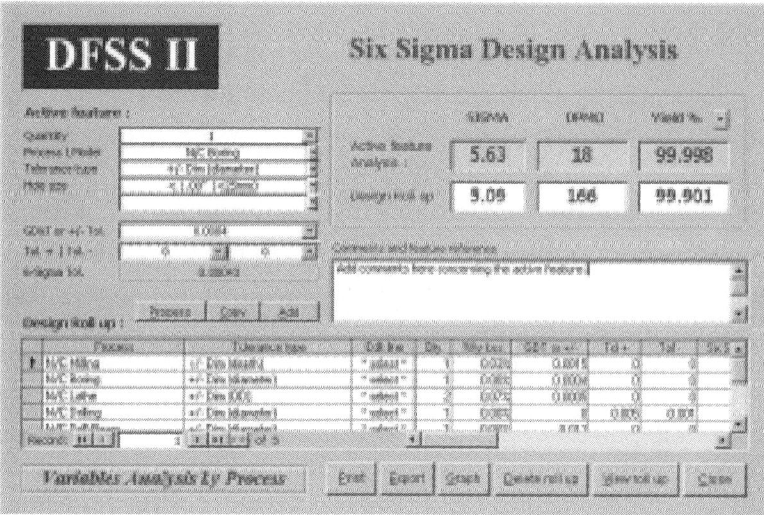

Reprinted with permission from Michael D. King, Ph.D., Sterling Technologies, Inc.

Figure 13-7. Process Capability Model Example

Figure 13-7 is a sample screen print of a process capability model from a commercially available DFSS tool. In Figure 13-7, the specific process and other manufacturing-related factors about the part feature being analyzed are selected by using the pull-down arrows under the *Active Feature* section of the model. Once the selections are made, the model displays the predicted yield, sigma value, and DPMO (defects per million opportunities rating) for producing the feature under the *Active Feature Analysis* section of the model. Based on these results, the company can make iterations by modifying the values among the factors, in order to achieve acceptable results. As each feature is analyzed following this procedure, the sigma value, DPMO summary, and overall yield for the design is displayed under the *Design Roll Up* section in the model. Using this methodology, process capability models play an integral role in helping a company achieve the ultimate DFSS goal of creating six sigma designs.

CASE STUDY

To illustrate the DFSS implementation process just described, consider the case of the Flow-Can Pump Company, which makes industrial-grade hydraulic pumps. Recently, Flow-Can was hired to develop a product for a new customer that it never worked with before. Based on Flow-Can's lack of familiarity with the customer, the company conducted a series of interviews with the customer to better understand the customer's wants and needs (DFSS process step 1).

Armed with this information and the specifications provided by the customer, Flow-Can proceeded to identify the product design requirements. To facilitate this activity, and to understand the relationship of the product requirements based on the customer input obtained through the interviews, Flow-Can elected to develop a QFD (quality function deployment) for this product. The results of this activity are shown in Figure 13-8.

With the knowledge gained from the QFD, Flow-Can proceeded to develop a product design solution that matched its customer's requirements (DFSS process step 2). As the QFD indicated, Flow-Can found out that leakage was the critical product requirement that affected customer satisfaction. To validate the integrity of the product design regarding leakage, Flow-Can created analytical models to determine the effects of leakage on pump performance. Through the analysis, Flow-Can was able to determine the maximum flow threshold the pump could endure without compromising the customer's requirement for leakage.

As the product development process proceeded into the detailed design phase, Flow-Can performed a cause-and-effects analysis to identify the individual part key characteristics that influence leakage. The results of the cause-and-effects analysis determined that the piston's outside diameter and the main

		Product Requirements				
Maximize, minimize, or target		Target	Max.	Max.	Target	Target
Customer Needs	**Importance Rating (1-Low, 10-High)**	Materials	Vibration	Leakage	Weight	Displacement
High Durability	4	7	10	4	4	7
Low Cost	7			4		7
High Reliability	4	7	7			7
High Performance	10		4	10		
Corrosion Free	1	10				
Relative Importance		66	108	144	16	105

Figure 13-8. Flow-Can's Quality Function Deployment

housing bore were the part features that caused pump leakage (DFSS process step 3).

As the design process evolved, Flow-Can conducted additional analyses to optimize its design by determining the appropriate fit condition between the piston and bore to minimize the effects of leakage. To facilitate this analysis, Flow-Can used process capability models to help determine tolerances for the individual part features (DFSS process step 4).

As this simple case study illustrates, a company can successfully implement DFSS only by integrating it with the product development process. DFSS can help reduce product variation by using data that provides insight into process capability. In summary, here are some key take-aways regarding DFSS:

- Variation in component design parameters can detract from the ability to meet a requirement.

- The probability of success in achieving design goals increases by properly managing variation in the design phase.
- Capability data and simulation techniques can be used early in the design phase to manage risk.

Design for Six Sigma is a methodology that proactively improves product quality through the design process. By using data and understanding the capability of the process, a company can prevent quality-related problems. Implementation of DFSS completes the quality pillar in the house of product development, as shown in Figure 13-9. Therefore, we can now turn to Chapter 14, our final chapter, and address how to synthesize the elements of the house of product development and achieve flow in the process.

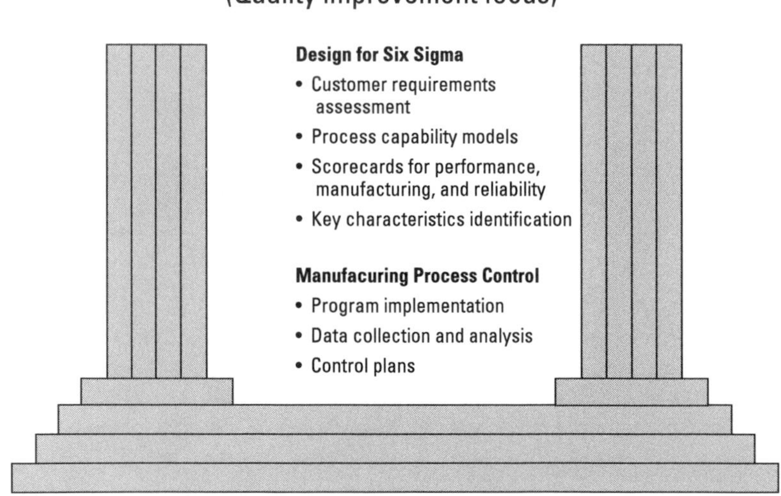

Figure 13-9. Completing the Quality Pillar

CHAPTER 14

Flow and Cell Design for Product Development

Chapter 2 discussed the concept of flow and its relationship to lean principles in terms of eliminating idle time and waste. Manufacturing facilitates flow by creating cells in which the product moves in a single-piece fashion from station to station. However, product development, as previously stated, deals with information, not parts. Consequently, the challenge in establishing flow in the product development arena deals with the movement of information from workstation to workstation.

Referring to the house of product development, implementation of a resource and workload management process (discussed in Chapter 6) is a foundational element in terms of process improvement, and a key initial step in establishing flow within product development. The workload management process initiates activity that strives to match work demand to capacity and manage work-in-progress (WIP), thereby minimizing the negative impacts of unplanned work, bottlenecks, multitasking, and expediting. However, to facilitate the establishment of flow within any process, it is necessary to introduce some additional lean concepts, specifically, concepts related to *takt time* and *standard work.*

MEASURING TAKT TIME

Takt time is defined as the available work time divided by the rate of customer demand. In other words, it represents the pace of a process that is matched to the demand of the customer. Takt time can be calculated using the following formula:

$$\text{Takt Time} = \frac{\text{Available Work Time}}{\text{Customer Demand}}$$

For example, let's say customer demand is 200 units per day and the factory operates at 8 hours (480 minutes) per day. Therefore, takt time would be 2.4 minutes (480 minutes / 200 units per day). In other words, in order to meet customer demand, the process must be capable of producing a unit every 2.4 minutes.

Takt time represents a bridge aligning the output of a process with customer demand, or, to use another term, the *pull* of the customer. If you recall the lean principals introduced in Chapter 2, one of the five principles (make value flow at the pull of the customer) is related to this issue of customer demand.

QUANTIFYING STANDARD WORK

Standard work defines the amount of work content performed by each worker within a process rate, in order to achieve a linear output rate. To accomplish this, the aggregate time for the series of work tasks to be performed for the product is equally dispersed among the workers so that an individual's task time - is equal to or less than the takt time. By achieving this, the daily output rate for the process is aligned with the customer demand.

This concept is illustrated in Figure 14-1. As shown in the graphic on the left, unbalanced worker task times lead to an unfavorable situation. In this case, Workers 2 and 3 are underutilized while Workers 1, 4, and 5 are over-utilized. Attempts to achieve flow with this arrangement would be unsuccessful. Based on the task time, a bottleneck would most likely develop

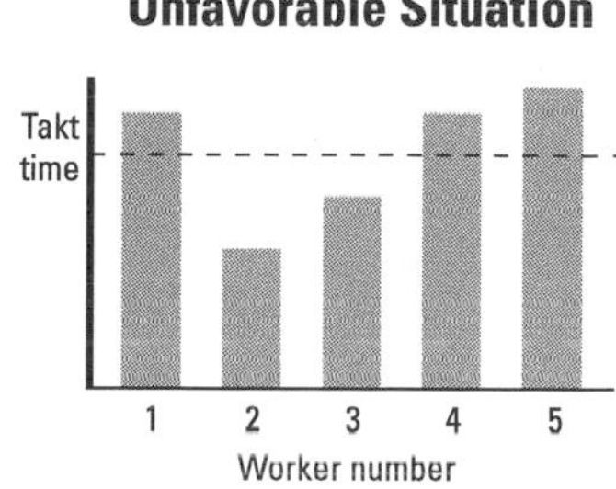

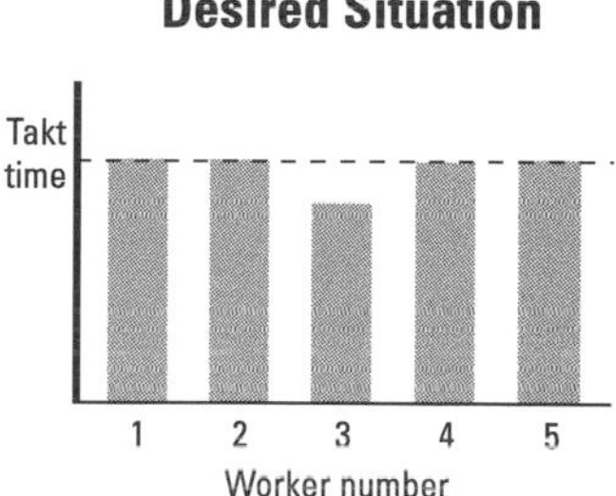

Figure 14-1. Balancing Work Allocation

in front of Worker 5. As a result, the pace and output of the entire process would be based on Worker 5's performance. This illustrates once again the theory of constraints introduced in Chapter 6.

In the graphic on the right, the task times for Workers 1, 2, 4, and 5 are equal and match the takt time while Worker 3 is slightly underutilized. This is an example of a desirable situation that is capable of achieving flow. With this arrangement, the handoff of all work in the process can occur at the same time, that is, the takt time. As a result, work could flow in a constant and continuous fashion with the process output equal to the takt time.

Standard work is a key enabler to facilitate flow. Based on its importance, here are some general characteristics regarding standard work:

- The importance of standard work must be recognized by everyone involved in the process.
- Standard work is based on observations of human motion.
- Standard work tasks must be fairly repetitive.
- The average worker must be able to perform standard work.
- Standard work is developed through a team approach.
- Standard work has some variance.
- There is always opportunity for improvement.

The concept of standard work has been employed extensively in the manufacturing arena to facilitate flow in the factory. In a flow environment, it is not uncommon for many individual work tasks to be completed in a relatively short period of time, typically, in terms of seconds or minutes. In the case of product development, however, many of the work tasks take considerably longer to complete, often hours. In this arena, the concept of standard work still applies, but it requires adapting and thinking about standard work in a different way. For example, a company can apply the standard work approach to completing an engineering stress analysis, creating an engineering blueprint drawing, or building a computer-aided design (CAD) model for a new product.

CELL DESIGN FOR PRODUCT DEVELOPMENT

A *cell* is defined as the co-location of people (skills) and equipment required to create a product. The manufacturing world facilitates flow by creating cells that are dedicated to manufacturing and assembling a specific family of products. Figure 14-2 is an example of a typical cell design employed in the factory.

As shown in Figure 14-2, with a cellular approach, the product moves from workstation to workstation in a U-shaped fashion. By leveraging standard work and takt time, each employee is able to complete the assigned task in conjunction with the other cell members. As a result, the movement of the product is sequenced at a constant rate, thereby achieving flow.

The cell concept is also adaptable within the product development process. However, because product development uses information instead of parts, it is not bound by the physical constraints required for the cellular approach in manufacturing. In manufacturing, the actual product passes from employee to employee. In product development, the concept of a cell can be facilitated through workstation hookups, with electronic triggers established between employees to provide signals for

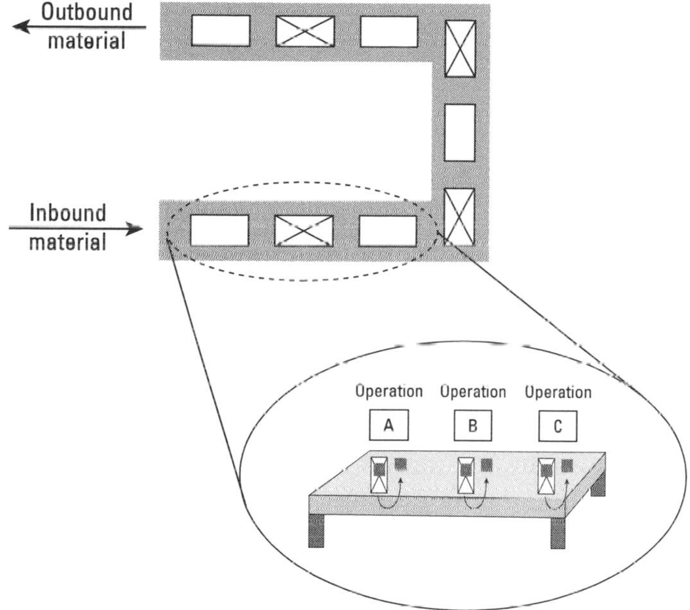

Figure 14-2. Typical Manufacturing Cell Layout

incoming work. Although it is still preferable to enhance communication and create a product development cell through the physical co-location of the employees involved in the process, using the approach of electronic links may be a more practical way to establish flow without the requirement of co-location.

Key steps necessary in the implementation of a product development cell are discussed in the following sections.

Step 1: Identify the Products to be Designed in the Cell

Similar to the approach of creating a cell within manufacturing, it is necessary to identify the products to be supported by the cell. This identification is a key enabler in leveraging standard work and standard processes for all of the products produced in the cell, and will facilitate flow.

Step 2: Develop an Information Database

Information is the basis for nearly all product development activities. Consequently, workers in the product development process require easy access to product information that is critical in supporting the process. The information database presented in Chapter 10 is an example of an information source that can be used to support the process.

Step 3: Consolidate Employee Skill Sets

Success in implementing a cellular approach in any environment is predicated on employees having the skills necessary to support the tasks required by the cell. As a result, implementation of a cell requires a review of the necessary skill sets and may require training and modification of job tasks to facilitate flow.

Achieving flow is the ultimate goal for implementing improvements in the product development process. However, implementing flow in a process that contains vast amounts of waste is not practical and would not benefit the company. Therefore, instituting the concepts of flow in product development is not advised until elements of a streamlined design process, and enablers to improve product quality, have been implemented. In terms of the house of product development, achieving flow is the last element to be implemented and consequently, represents the roof of the house (Figure 14-3).

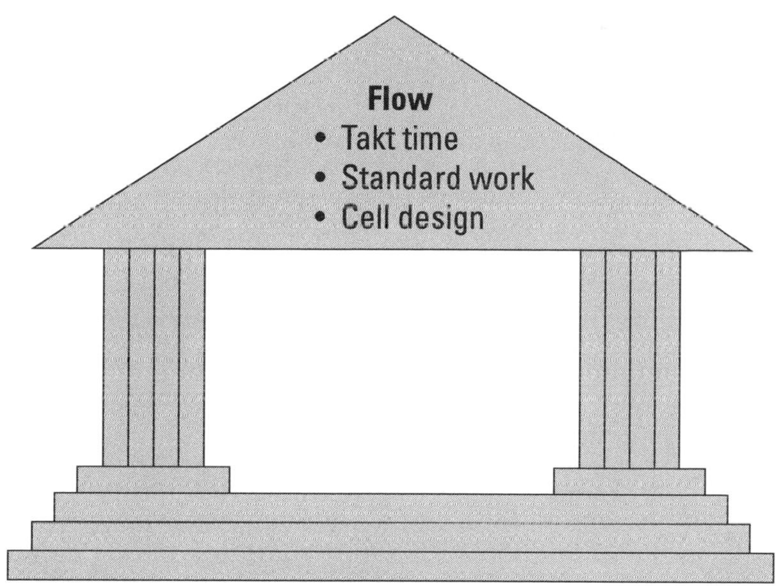

Figure 14-3. Adding the Roof

Conclusion

As a result of addressing each element associated with constructing the house of product development, the completed house is shown in Figure C-1. As you can see, the house is based on a comprehensive plan built on a strong foundation, including elements that address product development cycle time, product cost and quality, and provide value to the customer.

The foundational elements of resource and workload management, implementation of reuse concepts, and utilization of the correct level of process infrastructure are instrumental in providing order and stabilizing the product development process. In addition, these elements are instrumental in initiating the cultural changes in the organization that are needed to achieve real and sustained improvement. Once all of this is accomplished, improvement can proceed towards addressing the design process, the development of software systems, and integration of manufacturing and the company's supply chain. Collectively, these activities aid in streamlining the product development process and provide the benefit of reducing development cycle time and cost. Next, Manufacturing Process Control and Design for Six Sigma concepts are implemented with the goal of improving product quality. These elements utilize data as the basis for understanding process capabilities that can be leveraged to support new product design. Finally, flow is implemented through the creation of product development cells.

In terms of implementation, timing for many of the activities associated with a specific element overlap with activities from other elements. However, experience has demonstrated that companies that have followed the basic roadmap of implementation outlined by the house of product development have been able to maximize the benefits from their product development process.

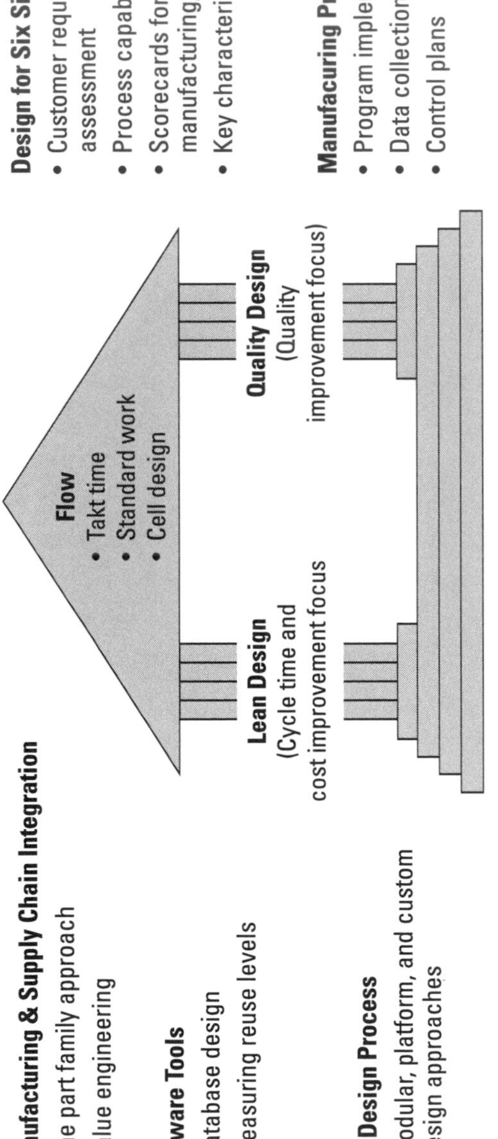

Figure C-1. The Completed House of Product Development

The application of lean and six sigma methodologies represents a powerful combination that can achieve dramatic results. Regarding product development, the three guiding ideas of working on what's important, concentrating the work, and reusing knowledge provide the backdrop that fuels the key elements for process improvement. Armed with this information, you are now ready to apply this knowledge within your own company and build your own house in order to achieve world-class performance from your product development process!

Glossary

Activity-Based Costing – An accounting method that allows a company to determine the actual cost associated with each product or service produced, independent of the company's overhead cost structure.

Attribute – A piece of information or characteristic that describes a part in some way.

Baseline Event – A comprehensive self-assessment used as the starting point to initiate process improvement. The objectives of the baseline event are to identify where problems exist, shape a vision for the future, determine where to start and what to do, and to solicit management commitment to proceed with an improvement plan.

Bottleneck – A condition occuring in a process when its incoming work level exceeds its output level.

Cell – The co-location of people (skills) and equipment required to process families of similar work, parts, or products.

Commodity Parts and Consumables – Parts represented in a company's product portfolio that are typically "off-the-shelf" items purchased by a company in support of the products they sell to their customers. Examples of these types of parts include nuts, bolts, diodes, capacitors, greases, lubricants, etc.

Component Design Compliance Matrix – A product development tool that identifies design requirements, criteria, verification and validation methods, and current experience levels for an individual component. This tool assists in developing actions when component designs do not meet minimum technical requirements.

Concurrent Engineering – A systematic approach to the integrated, concurrent design of products and their related processes, including manufacturing and support.

Critical-To-Quality (CTQ) Characteristic – A term used to define one of the select few characteristics of a product, which has a significant impact on product performance or customer satisfaction.

Custom Design – A product development approach that is utilized to expand the company's product portfolio. Compared against the product development continuum, the custom design approach represents the highest level of risk and lowest level of reuse.

Design for Six Sigma (DFSS) – A methodology to manage and reduce variation in the product design process while meeting all customer expectations and producing products at six sigma quality levels.

Five-S (5S) – A methodology to transform and maintain a work environment that supports lean implementation. In addition, it promotes a culture of discipline and efficiency in the workplace. The term "five S" is derived from Japanese words meaning sort, store, shine, standardize, and sustain.

Flow – The continuous movement of products and information through a value stream.

Group Technology – A management philosophy based on leveraging similarities in the design and manufacture of parts for the purpose of performing a known function.

Key Characteristic – A feature of a part whose variation has significant influence on product fit, performance, reliability, manufacturing, or cost.

Lean – A philosophy of producing what is needed, when it is needed, with the minimum amount of time, resources, and space.

Manufacturing Process Control (MPC) – An approach that assesses part variability by analyzing measurement data. This is accomplished by controlling the process parameters that influence the manufacture of the part features.

Modular Design – A product development approach that is based on using modules/subassemblies for new product design. Compared against the product development continuum, the modular design approach represents the highest level of reuse and lowest level of risk.

Module – A term for a subassembly representing high reuse potential. Typically, modules are used in conjunction with the modular design approach.

Multitasking – The concept of working multiple jobs concurrently. Leads to bottlenecks in the value stream and higher degrees of inefficiency and human error.

Non-Value-Added Activity – An activity that does not meet all three criteria of a value-added activity. In other words, an activity that utilizes time or resources, but does not meet the customer's requirements.

Part Family – A grouping of parts with similar characteristics.

Platform Design – A product development approach that is based on using a platform or baseline product for a new product design. The key objective of the platform design approach is to understand and manage the technical risk.

Preferred Part – A designation linked to a part design that is promoted for reuse. The criteria for selecting a preferred part are based on engineering, manufacturing, and business considerations unique to a specific part family.

Process Capability Model – An analytical tool that uses historical data for predicting the sigma value for producing a part feature. The sigma value determined by the model is based on the manufacturing process used to produce the feature, as well as other factors such as the material type, feature size, tolerance, and so on.

Product Breakdown Structure – A product development tool that "breaks down" a product into smaller and smaller pieces. Essentially, it is a tree diagram that starts at the product level, then the product is further subdivided into major assemblies, modules/subassemblies, and finally detail parts. The key objective of this tool is to identify opportunities for part/module reuse.

Product Experience Domain – A product development tool that identifies design parameters essential to product performance, quality, and reliability. Information can be provided in various forms, including cataloged data, tables, and graphics. This tool proactively identifies risk by identifying areas where product experience exists.

Product Portfolio – The collection of all of the products and parts managed by a company.

Product Scorecard – A software tool used for determining the sigma score of a product's capability with regard to its performance, manufacturing capability, and reliability.

Product-Specific Parts – Parts represented in a company's product portfolio that are typically designed and produced by the company in support of the products they sell to their customers.

Reuse Process – A process that leverages a company's existing product portfolio through the use of attribute data, preferred parts, and software tools, to identify parts with high reuse potential in support of new product design.

Sigma – A term that represents standard deviation. Standard deviation is defined as the measure of variation or "scatter" in a process.

Standard Work – Prescribed work tasks performed by workers in a process in order to achieve a linear output rate that matches takt time.

Takt Time – The available work time divided by the rate of the customer demand. In other words, it represents the "pace" of the process output that is matched to the demand of the customer.

Technical Requirements Flow-Down Matrix – A product development tool that identifies product technical requirements, description, recommendations, priority, assumptions, and key affected components. When referenced against a baseline product, components affected by noncompliance are noted.

Theory of Constraints – A theory that contends the overall output of any process is limited, or constrained, by the least productive step in the process.

Time-Value Map – A tool that provides a graphical assessment of value-added and non-value-added time in a process.

Total Quality Leadership (TQL) – A continuous improvement initiative that strives to manage an organization so that every job and every process is carried out correctly, the first time and every time.

Value-Added Activity – An activity that (1) changes the form, fit, or function of the material or information, (2) is done correctly the first time, and (3) is something the customer is willing to pay for. All three criteria must be met for an activity to be considered value-added.

Value Engineering – A methodology to reduce product cost through a collaborative effort between a company and its parts provider, for their mutual benefit.

Value Stream – The sequence of all of the value-added and non-value-added activities that are necessary for producing a product.

Value Stream Map – A lean tool that documents the sequence and flow of the activities associated with producing a product. A key objective of this tool is to aid in identifying areas of waste that represent improvement opportunities.

Waste – Another term associated with non-value-added activities. Under the lean philosophy, waste can be grouped into seven different categories: defects, overproduction, inventory, motion, processing, transportation, and waiting.

References

Fiore, Clifford. *Lean Strategies for Product Development: Achieving Breakthrough Performance in Bringing Products to Market*. Milwaukee, WI: ASQ Quality Press, 2003.

Hines, Peter, and David Taylor. *Going Lean: A Guide to Implementation*. Available from: Lean Enterprise Research Centre, Aberconway Building, Colum Drive, Cardiff CF10 3EU, UK.

Hirano, Hiroyuki. *5 Pillars of the Visual Workplace: The Sourcebook for 5S Implementation*. Portland, OR: Productivity Press, 1995.

Rother, Mike, and John Shook. *Learning to See: Value Stream Mapping to Add Value and Eliminate Muda*. Brookline, MA: The Lean Enterprise Institute, 1998.

Swartz, James B. *The Hunters and the Hunted: A Non-Linear Solution for Reengineering the Workplace*. New York: Productivity Press, 1994.

Taylor, David, and David Brunt. *Manufacturing Operations and Supply Chain Management: The Lean Approach*. Stamford, CT: Thomson Learning, 2001.

Womack, James P., and Daniel T. Jones. *Lean Thinking: Banish Waste and Create Wealth in Your Corporation*. New York, Simon & Schuster, 1996.

Womack, James P., Daniel T. Jones, and Daniel Roos. *The Machine That Changed the World*. New York: Rawson Associates, 1990.

Index

About the Author

Clifford Fiore is a certified black belt and lean expert and has been employed with Honeywell International for the past 18 years. He is recognized as an industry leader in implementing concepts towards reducing product cost and development cycle times with extensive experience in design, manufacturing, process improvement, and quality improvement. He has an MBA in Technology Management and holds a senior level certification from the American Society of Mechanical Engineers in Geometric Dimensioning & Tolerencing.